NORTH WALES
MURDER
CASEBOOK

STEVE FIELDING

COUNTRYSIDE BOOKS
NEWBURY   BERKSHIRE

CW00456348

First published 1995
© Steve Fielding 1995

All rights reserved. No reproduction
permitted without the prior permission
of the publishers:

COUNTRYSIDE BOOKS
3 Catherine Road
Newbury, Berkshire

ISBN 1 85306 380 0

Designed by Mon Mohan

Produced through MRM Associates Ltd., Reading
Typeset by Textype, Cambridge
Printed by Woolnough Bookbinding Ltd., Irthlingborough

Contents

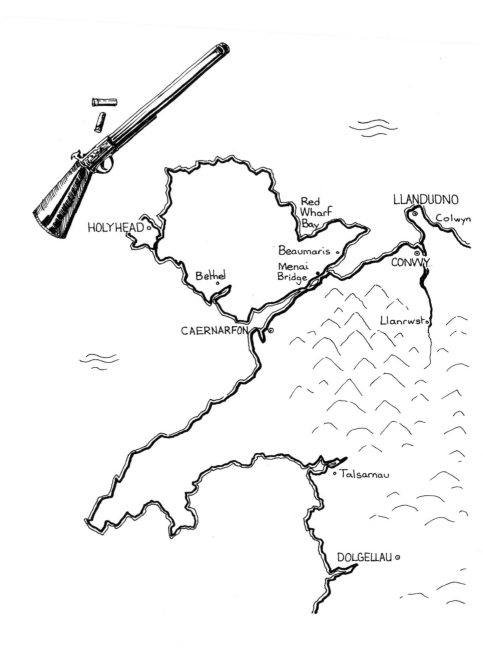

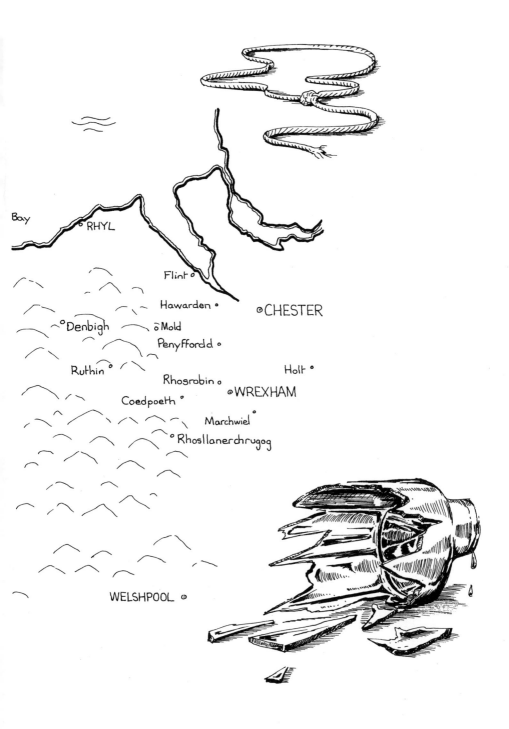

INTRODUCTION

The foundations of our modern British police force date back to 1829. Following the pioneering work of Home Secretary Robert Peel in setting up a Metropolitan police force in London, other regions quickly followed suit. In 1835 Parliament passed the Muncipal Corporation Act which encouraged boroughs of a certain population to establish their own forces, and in 1839 a further Act was passed allowing the formation of county constabularies.

The first county in North Wales to take this initiative was Denbighshire and early in 1840 the Denbighshire police force headquarters was set up at Ruthin. In 1842, the Parish Constables Act was passed with the intention of turning the hitherto poorly paid parish constables into a disciplined body of men.

By the mid 19th century many parts of the British Isles were in the grip of the industrial revolution. Besides bringing new technology, wealth and other benefits, the revolution also brought with it many new problems. Previously peaceful hamlets found themselves invaded by 'foreigners' seeking work. It was soon clear that the old-fashioned parish constables could not cope with the rising tide of crime and as a result many other parts of North Wales followed Denbighshire's lead and set up their own forces.

Immigrant workers travelled to North Wales from Ireland and Scotland and across the border from Liverpool and Cheshire. Employment was to be had both in the numerous mines and in the new railways that were under construction, such as the Ffestiniog to Porthmadog and Holyhead to Chester lines. Towns close to both these proposed lines played host to hordes of navvies and on more than one occasion the police were forced to stand by helpless as large drunken gangs of English and Irish workers staged pitched battles.

Other types of crimes were also prevalent: prostitution, alcoholism and vagrancy were common offences, as were numerous crimes against people and property. Punishments were tough and severe penalties could be and often were inflicted for relatively minor offences. That said, North Wales had a record of being a safe place in which to live and work.

By the 1880s the various police forces had become established as efficient and effective law enforcers. In 1888 the Local Government Act was passed, which saw the formation of county councils. There was a certain amount of disquiet at this encroachment on their powers amongst the country gentry who had overseen the early development of the police forces. The solution found was to grant these gentry folk positions on joint standing committees administering the county force alongside and in partnership with elected county authorities.

The technological revolution of the 20th century was to provide many great aids to police work. Fingerprinting became an established and proven method of identification in 1905 and the motor car was quickly utilised by most police forces.

Murder is a heinous crime and for most of us, thankfully, the closest we will get is through the pages of this book. North Wales has nevertheless played host to many sensational cases.

Extracts from the early records show that on 2nd May 1751, a preacher was hanged at the Marsh (Morfa Seiont), Caernarfon, for the murder of his wife by striking her with a shoemaker's hammer and afterwards throwing her into the mill pond of Felin Bach, near Glangwna. The executioner was a man named Symon, who travelled from his home at Clocaenog, near Denbigh, to carry out the sentence. Other notable early crimes include the murder of John Tibbott by his son William at Llanllwchaiarn in 1830. It was alleged that the son had mixed eight drachms of arsenic in his father's food. Tibbott was hanged in front of the old gaol above the market place at Montgomery.

In 1868, following a number of major disturbances at public executions, a law was passed that decreed all executions should take place inside prisons. This had not been the case when Richard Rowlands was hanged outside Beaumaris Castle in 1862, in the last public execution in North Wales. The stories of the last two men hanged in North Wales are both contained in this casebook.

Many of the following cases were well documented across the whole of Great Britain, two examples being the murder of Sarah Hughes by Cadwaladr Jones at Dolgellau in 1877, and more recently the horrific discovery of a 'mummy' in a quiet Rhyl boarding house.

The region also has links with other notorious murderers. Ruth Ellis, the infamous nightclub hostess who blasted her lover to death in a London street, and who history records as the last woman to be hanged in Britain, was a native of Rhyl, and the quiet seaside town was also involved in one of the most controversial murder cases of the 20th century. In early 1962, James Hanratty was arrested for what was known as the A6 murder. At his trial Hanratty foolishly changed his alibi halfway through proceedings and said that he could not have committed the murder as he was staying at a Rhyl guest house. Several witnesses from the town supported this, but he was convicted and hanged at Bedford in April. The case still causes controversy and many people believe an innocent man went to the gallows.

The Life, Trial, and

EXECUTION,

Of William TIBBOT,

Who was Executed at Montgomery, on Monday last, August 16th, 1830,

FOR THE

WILFUL MURDER,

Of HIS FATHER, John Tibbot,

———o——ooo——o———

WILLIAM TIBBOT, aged 40, the wretched man executed on Monday Morning last, was capitally convicted at the Great Session at Welch-Pool, for the county of Montgomery, of the horrible Murder of his own Father. He effected his guilty and horrible purpose by poison, which he purchased in a shop at Montgomery; he was a native of Llanwllchairn. It appeared by the evidence that the deceased was proprietor of the house jointly occupied by himself and the prisoner, his Son; that in consequence of his Son not paying him the rent, the deceased caused a distress to be made, and afterwards an ejectment to be served upon the unfortunate prisoner, who said that before the Sessions came he would kill his Father. The prisoner pleaded not guilty, but after a long, painfull, and full investigation of the case, and upon the clearest circumstantial evidence, he was by an impartial and intelligent Jury pronounced Guilty of Murder. The learned Judge in proceeding to pass sentence, said, that he the prisoner at the bar, had been found guilty of a most foul and horrible Murder, committed upon his own Father---that the laws of God and man required that when man shed another's blood, by man should his blood be shed :---he exhorted him in a most feeling manner to prepare himself for that awful fate which awaited him, and to seek peace with that God whom he had so greatly offended ; that all mercy was denied him on earth ; and he hoped the prisoner would so attend to the admonitions and advice of the Divine, who would attend him the few short hours he had to remain on earth, that he may receive that pardon from God, which the offended laws of his country could not extend to him.

He appeared very firm during the trial, and repeatedly denied his guilt, but has since confessed that he bought the poison, and that his wife administered it in Tea, and confessed the Murder of his former wife some years ago, in the same manner. When he ascended the scaffold, he seemed very penetent, and was twice heard to exclaim, "Lord have mercy on me"—and was launched into awful eternity.

Sinners by my example and awful death warning; and listen to the admonition of a dying man—turn from the error of your ways and seek the Lord while he may be found,

Hark ! 'tis the dreary midnight bell That breaks the gloom profound ; It seems to toll my funeral knell, How dismal is the sound.	When Cain his brother's blood did spill 'Twas passion bore the sway, . But worse than Cain, in spite most fell, I took his life away.
A few short hours, and I must stand Exposed to shame and scorn ; Ah, sad and luckless was the day That ever I was born.	Most gracious God, tho' just, yet kind, With pity look on me, And grant that I may mercy find Though on the Gallows tree.
The hand of Heaven is clearly seen In this most awful case ; The murderer he will not screen, But bring him to disgrace.	I hope no person will reflect On those I've left behind, My offsprings quite unconscious Of this, my wicked crime.
Few are the hours I've now to live, How swift the moments fly ; Oh Heav'nly power ! assistance give Upon the day I die.	I hope you will a warning take, All you who come to spy, The wretched end of me you'll see, All on a gallows high.

France, Printer, Mardol, Shrewsbury.

Broadsheet lamenting the execution of William Tibbott, at Montgomery.

The police force as we know it today took shape in 1950 when the forces of Anglesey, Caernarfonshire and Merionethshire were merged to become the Gwynedd Constabulary. A Royal Commission report into the running of the police forces, in the early 1960s, recommended that many of the smaller forces combine, and in 1967 Gwynedd was amalgamated with the forces of Denbighshire and Flintshire, retaining the name Gwynedd Constabulary. The strength of the new force was a little over 1,000 serving officers with another 200 civilian workers.

The force relocated to the new headquarters at Colwyn Bay in late 1973, and six months later when the restructuring of local government saw the radical redrawing of many county boundaries, the force was renamed North Wales Police (Heddlu Gogledd Cymru).

Research has shown that the streets of North Wales are amongst the safest in Great Britain, thanks in no small way to the endeavours of the North Wales police force.

Steve Fielding
Autumn 1995

1

THE SECRET SINNER

THE MURDER OF SARAH HUGHES AT DOLGELLAU,
JUNE 1877

Shortly after dawn on the morning of 16th July 1877, a young girl out
walking at Dolgellau spotted a human arm floating in the fast
flowing waters of the river Arran and hurried home to tell her parents.
They in turn alerted the police, and soon a vast crowd of people had
congregated along the riverbank as, under the watchful eye of Chief
Constable Clough, officers from the Merionethshire police force joined
the local police in searching the river and its bank for clues.

As the search was stepped up more grisly remains were discovered. A
weaver at the Aberneient factory, one of many that stood along the
riverbank, found the lower part of a female torso, and a short time later
a worker at another local factory found a dismembered foot – still
inside a boot – and a little further downstream he pulled out a head. It
had been crudely butchered, seeming to hamper identification: all traces
of hair had been cropped away, the eyes had been removed from their
sockets, and the jaw and cheek bones had been staved in.

Soon workers from another nearby factory made their own gruesome
discoveries. First, part of leg, then a thigh, items of clothing, a right
arm. . . the gory list continued.

Later that afternoon as the collection of body parts was transferred
to the local workhouse, a surgeon reconstructed them like some
macabre jigsaw puzzle. It was soon clear that the body was that of a
woman. All major parts of the body had been found with exception of
part of the right leg. The crude dissection had evidently been carried out
with an axe. It was not the work of a skilled butcher, as there were
several axe marks where the killer had made unsuccessful cuts close to
the main severance points.

Identification was provided by Miss Margaret Hughes who,
accompanied by her father, told police that the body was that of her
sister Sarah Hughes, who had been reported missing a few weeks
before.

How the *Illustrated News* depicted the murder of Sarah Hughes.

Thirty six year old Sarah Hughes was the unmarried mother of two children; not unusual in today's liberal society, but to many strait-laced folk of the last century an unmarried mother was often no better than a prostitute, and Margaret Hughes had been faced with this puritanical prejudice when she first reported her sister missing.

On the afternoon of Thursday, 4th June, Sarah had left her home at Brithdir travelling to Dolgellau, a trip of some four miles. She had been wearing a black silk dress, red stockings and a felt jacket. She reached her destination later that afternoon and called on a number of friends and relatives before setting off on the return journey shortly after 9 pm. She never reached her home.

Margaret became worried when Sarah failed to return, and voiced her fears to her parents that something was wrong. Soon a search party was out scouring the tracks Sarah would have walked on her way home.

The police were informed but seemed to be of the opinion that she had run off with a man – the assumption being made on the preconception that Sarah Hughes was a woman of low morals. The family's pleadings that she could be in danger, or worse, fell on deaf ears, and while a token gesture – to contact other forces in the south – was made, the police authorities showed little interest in carrying out their own investigations. Undeterred, the Hughes family carried on the search for Sarah, and six weeks later their wait was over.

Officers who had hitherto displayed little interest in the search suddenly sprang into action. Once a positive identification had been made, they set about calculating the date when the body was placed into the water.

The first piece of luck was being able to pinpoint the time down to the last two days. Prior to this the river had been very low, due to a long dry spell which had ended on 14th July, when there had been a terrific downpour. Police reasoned that if the body had been in the river earlier, it would have been seen by one of the many local anglers who fished the water, and others who picnicked or rambled in the area.

Working on the theory that whoever had tossed the remains into the water had done so recently, suggested that Sarah must have been killed and her body concealed close by. This was a twofold theory. Firstly, it was hard to imagine that Sarah would not have been spotted, bearing in mind the intensive search her family made; and secondly, the killer or killers would surely not have risked carrying a dismembered body along a fairly well used track, whatever time of day or night. On this assumption, police officers surmised the killer must be a local and set about interviewing the people of Dolgellau and the surrounding area.

On the afternoon of 17th July, as Sarah Hughes was buried at Brithdir cemetery, police questioned Cadwaladr Jones.

Cadwaladr Jones was a 26 year old family man who ran the successful Parc Farm on the outskirts of Dolgellau. The farm stood adjacent to a ravine that flowed into the river Arran close to where witnesses had found parts of the dismembered torso, and near to the route Sarah Hughes would have walked on that fateful night.

Sarah's father had expressed a fear of Jones's involvement in the crime and police soon learned there was a connection between Jones and the dead woman. Sarah supplemented her income, which mainly came from taking in washing, by doing some casual work at nearby Coed Mwsoglog Farm, a place where Jones also worked some of the time, usually mid-week, often sleeping on the premises.

A witness saw Jones close to the route Sarah would have taken on her way home from Dolgellau on 4th June. Then it was learned that Jones's wife had been away from their home on that night. Had Jones and Sarah Hughes been having an affair? Was it a coincidence that he chose to spend that Thursday at home? Had they planned a secret assignation?

Soon, the evidence against Cadwaladr Jones built up. Witnesses came forward to say that Jones had been seen fishing in the river on the morning that the first severed limbs were discovered. This aroused suspicion in one witness who was aware that Jones should have been at work on the farm when instead he was idling by the river.

Cadwaladr Jones committed the brutal murder in the shadow of the picturesque Cadair Idris.

Next morning a number of officers surrounded Jones's farmhouse and waited for him to emerge. An hour later Cadwaladr stepped outside and Inspector Jones spoke to him. 'Do you object if we search the farm?' the inspector asked, adding that he was not being singled out and that every neighbouring farmer would be paid a visit in due course.

The visit must have rattled Jones for shortly after he spoke to a sergeant and asked if he could speak with the inspector alone. 'You need not trouble yourself any further. I did it,' he said.

Jones was placed under arrest and then he led them around the farm, pointing out various items of clothing. At one point he pulled back some branches and uncovered a fingernail with some flesh attached.

Jones was removed to Dolgellau police station while officers returned to the farm for a more intensive search. They uncovered a shallow grave which had evidently been where Sarah Hughes had lain until Jones had decided to dismember her body and scatter the remains in the river.

When Jones stood trial at Chester Assizes it became clear that Sarah Hughes had indeed been his mistress. They had carried on the affair for a time until she announced she was pregnant. Fearful of losing his standing as a highly respected member of the community, Jones calmly decided to rid himself of the unwanted burden, not only of a bastard child, but of a lover of whom he had grown tired and who was starting to make life awkward for him.

His defence denied this and claimed that Jones and Sarah had merely been having a quarrel and in a fit of temper he had struck and accidentally killed her. In a panic he decided upon dismembering her to conceal all trace of the crime.

He was condemned to be hanged on 23rd November 1877, and a gallows was brought from Chester Castle for Hangman William Marwood to carry out the sentence.

Jones spent his last night in the company of a local clergyman and after the execution was carried out, the local newspaper stated that he had confessed: 'I intended to kill Sarah Hughes, more's the pity.' Asked when he decided on this, Jones confirmed that it was a couple of days before he carried it out.

The last word on the sordid tragedy must go a local newspaper whose account of the crime ended with the warning: 'Cadwaladr Jones's case is an atrocious, daring, despicable revelation and his execution the close of a career of secret sinning.'

2

A JUG OF STOUT

THE MURDER OF WILLIAM MABBOTS AT WELSHPOOL,
JUNE 1886

Strychnine is a particularly violent poison. First discovered in 1817, and derived from the ripened seeds of the tree *Strychnos nux vomica*, found predominantly in India, it was initially made available to the general public in both medicine form and as a vermin killer.

In small measured doses strychnine can act as a stimulant and was a common ingredient in certain tonics and pick-me-ups popular in the late 19th and early 20th centuries. Larger doses, though, have the opposite effect. Rapidly absorbed into the bloodstream, strychnine causes violent spasms in the body and quickly leads to a general breakdown of both the respiratory and central nervous system. Death usually comes within the hour, but not before the victim has suffered great agony.

It was not long after its introduction before the poison found its way into the hands of the criminal fraternity. Although both colourless and odourless, it has a bitter taste which the poisoner would often try to conceal. Notorious criminals have administered strychnine disguised in such things as brandy, jam and health salts.

On Monday, 14th June 1886, 37 year old William Mabbots left his wife and three children at home in Shrewsbury and travelled to his workplace at Welshpool. Mabbots had been in the grocery trade all his working life and was currently the branch manager of Messrs Debac and Sheaff, wholesale grocers, on Church Street, Welshpool, a position he had held for four years.

Mabbots had taken the position at Welshpool after leaving his own business in Shrewsbury, and his routine was such that he divided his time between working in the Welshpool shop on Saturdays and Mondays, the only days of the week the shop opened, and running the company's stall on Newtown market for the rest of the week.

The Welshpool shop was tenanted by Messrs Debac and Sheaff and came with a unfurnished house. Mabbots had a bed made up in one of the rooms in the house and often slept there on Monday nights, choosing to depart for Newtown from Welshpool rather than his home in Shrewsbury.

Five years earlier, a William Samuels, then aged 19, had also entered employment with Messrs Debac and Sheaff at Welshpool. He had been with the firm for a little over a year when William Mabbots joined as manager. He had stayed for one year and then moved on.

Three years later their paths crossed again when Samuels went into business on his own, running a market stall at Welshpool. He took an account at Debac and Sheaff, who supplied him with wholesale items such as tea and other goods.

During the late spring of 1886, Samuels began to get into debt with his account and Mabbots was instructed by his superiors to take steps to reclaim some of the money owed, which stood at one stage at £7 11s. There appeared to be no animosity between the two men and when asked by Mabbots, Samuels began to repay the money in instalments. On 12th June, Samuels made another payment which left a balance of 16 shillings.

On Monday 14th June, Samuels entered the shop late in the afternoon. He did not purchase anything and the errand boy later testified that he was unsure why he should have come into the shop without reason. Mabbots chatted with Samuels for a time before asking when he would be able to settle his account.

Samuels gave a vague answer but mentioned he would return after tea and sort it out. He left the shop and returned a short time later carrying a jug of ale. Samuels offered a glass of the porter to Mabbots and he accepted. They talked for a while then Samuels bade him farewell and left.

Tommy Morris, the young errand boy, was busying himself in the shop when Mabbots was suddenly taken ill. 'What has Samuels given me? I wish I had never seen him' he cried, collapsing on the floor. Morris was sent to fetch help and soon a crowd congregated in the shop front. Mabbots seemed to be having a fit and was obviously in agony.

At 6.40 pm, Dr Marston arrived and arranged for a stomach pump to be fetched while he administered an emetic. Mabbots was violently sick following the emetic and in a great deal of pain. After suffering further convulsions he died at seven o'clock. Right up until almost the moment of his death, he blamed Samuels for making him ill.

Samuels by this time had returned to the shop in the company of two men. He seemed to be at great pains to show that his companions had drunk from the jug with no ill effects. However, the jug was examined by two local doctors, who noticed clear traces of strychnine. Samuels was then taken to the police station, questioned and later charged with murder.

On Thursday, 8th July 1886, the sensational trial of William Samuels

THE
WELSHPOOL TRAGEDY.

NARRATIVE OF THE CASE.

THE PRISONER SAMUELS IN THE DOCK.

EXECUTION
OF
WILLIAM SAMUELS
AT SHREWSBURY.

CONFESSION OF THE PRISONER.

SHREWSBURY, Monday Morning.

Happily for nearly twenty years this part of the country has been free from any crime which has necessitated the carrying out of the most severe penalty of the law within the precincts of Shrewsbury Gaol, and if there be any satisfaction in the present case it is the knowledge that although the victim in the present instance is a Shrewsbury man, yet the crime itself was committed in a neighbouring county. A few years back the Government undertook the charge of the prisons, and the result has been that the number of prisons has from economical reasons been diminished, and the old prison on the Dana now finds accommodation for all the prisoners committed both in Shropshire and Montgomeryshire. Through this arrangement the prisoner William Samuels, when committed for trial by the Welshpool magistrates, was sent to her Majesty's prison at Shrewsbury, and since the sentence he was again incarcerated within its walls; and here to-day the sentence of the judge was duly carried out.

Contemporary newspaper headline on the execution of the Welshpool poisoner.

opened at Montgomeryshire Midsummer Assizes at Newtown. Mr Justice Groves presided over events which were witnessed by a crowd squeezed to capacity in the town's public rooms.

The opening day of the trial was devoted to the prosecution who set about proving that William Samuels was guilty of a callously premeditated murder, and that William Mabbots had been secretly, and for little reason, marked down as the victim of his deadly hatred.

Numerous witnesses gave evidence of that day's events. Samuels was seen to leave Mabbots' shop carrying an empty white jug and enter the Bull Hotel at six o'clock. He purchased a pint of stout which was drawn into the jug. He paid the licensee's wife, Mrs Eliza Jones, and left.

Later that evening Samuels had returned to the Bull Hotel and asked Mrs Jones if she remembered selling him the draft of ale for the man in the tea shop who was now very ill. Mrs Jones certainly recalled selling the ale although she was adamant that he had never said who the jug was intended for. Samuels had paid for it in coppers.

A witness named Arthur Gough then testified that he had bumped into Samuels as he emerged from the Bull. Seeing he was carrying the ale, Gough said to him, 'Good health, William,' to which Samuels responded by offering both Gough and Ben Slim, a friend of Gough, a swig from the jug, which both partook of to no ill effect.

The prosecution alleged that Samuels had added the poison to the jug after leaving the Bull. From the several testimonies given that day it seemed clear that Samuels had been alone for a short period of time between leaving the Bull and entering the shop.

On the following day medical evidence was given by two local surgeons, Dr Hawksworth and Dr Marston who recalled how they attended the scene and immediately suspected strychnine poisoning. Tests in their laboratories found this to be the case.

The most damning evidence against Samuels was supplied by two fellow market traders who testified that they had been asked by the accused to obtain some rat poison a week before the murder. George Ellis told the court how he was approached to buy some strychnine for Samuels to kill rats. Along with a friend, Ellis called at a local chemist but the manager was suspicious and refused to sell to the men.

Samuels also asked another youth to buy the poison, saying it was for someone at the railway yard who was having trouble with rats in the engine shed, but the lad refused. Samuels eventually duped a friend into buying it, saying it was for a gardener who was having trouble with vermin.

Counsel for the defence, realising the strength of the prosecution case, tried to counter the charge by claiming that the victim had either administered the poison himself, thereby committing suicide, or it had gotten into the porter by accident. Neither conjecture stood up to the facts and it was a weak and unsubstantiated plea.

Summing up the case, Mr Justice Groves pointed out the key points to the jury. They were asked to be sure they were satisfied as to the prisoner's guilt on the evidence read before them. The judge pointed to the lack of a clear motive, other than that the prisoner owed some money which Mabbots had been instructed to collect. However, Samuels had tried, days before the crime, several times to buy strychnine, which he had finally succeeded in doing. Samuels was also seen to bring into the shop a jug of ale, iden-tified as containing strychnine and from which Mabbots drank before collapsing in agony.

Retiring, the jury took little over 20 minutes to find Samuels guilty of murder and he was sentenced to death.

Transferred from Newtown to Shrewsbury via Welshpool, Samuels had to run the gauntlet of hatred by the townsfolk and at one stage he was struck on the head as he changed trains.

From the moment of his arrest until the evening prior to his execution, almost two months later, Samuels maintained he was innocent of the crime for which he was about to die. Finally, at 10.30 pm on Sunday night, 25th July, Samuels burst into tears and asked to speak to the governor of Shrewsbury prison. Without stating a motive, Samuels admitted that he had indeed purchased poison which he intended to administer to William Mabbots and that he had carried out the crime as the prosecution had stated at the trial. He expressed great regret for what he had done and acknowledged the sentence as a just one.

There had not been an execution at Shrewsbury for 20 years and a large crowd assembled outside the prison walls on Monday morning, 26th July 1886 as a bell tolled its dismal death knell for William Samuels. On the stroke of 8 am, Samuels walked to the scaffold unaided, where he was dispatched quickly by hangman James Berry.

3

A JEALOUS MAN

THE MURDER OF SIAN HUGHES AT RHOSROBIN,
NOVEMBER 1902

The burning embers of the previous night's bonfires still glowed in the chilly morning air as William Hughes walked free from Shrewsbury prison. It was Thursday, 6th November 1902, and as the heavy gates closed behind him, Hughes was in a rage. The 43 year old miner had just finished a three month stretch with hard labour, imposed upon him for deserting his wife and family. It was the culmination of a domestic dispute that was to have terrible consequences.

Hughes was born into a well respected Denbighshire family. He worked as a farmer upon leaving school before enlisting in the Second Battalion Cheshire Regiment, a military career that saw him spend most of his service in India.

In 1890, after serving eleven years, Hughes returned to civvy street and instead of returning to the family's Denbigh home, he settled in Wrexham, finding work in one of the many local coal mines.

Two years later he married Jane Hannah Williams, who preferred to be known as 'Sian'. She was his first cousin and some ten years his junior. They had five children, of whom two died in infancy, and although outwardly they seemed a happy family, the parents' relationship was fraught with quarrels, unhappiness and misfortune.

In 1900, Hughes deserted his wife and children and fled to Birkenhead where he found a job and took lodgings. Sian followed him across the border and they were reconciled, opting to stay in Birkenhead. In the following year Sian gave birth to a child which later died, and after a short stay in the Chester infirmary the couple decided to relocate back to Wrexham, finding a house at Pierce's Square, Pentrefelin, where later that year tragedy struck again when their six year old daughter passed away.

Within a few days of his daughter's funeral, Hughes again walked out on his wife. This time, instead of following her husband as before, Sian

THE
RHOSROBIN MURDER.

TRIAL OF WILLIAM HUGHES.

INSANITY THE DEFENCE.

VERDICT OF GUILTY & SENTENCE OF DEATH.

OPENING AND CLOSING SCENES.

The scene of the crime.

William Hughes as sketched in court. (*Al Davies*)

Hughes threw herself on the mercy of the Wrexham Board of Guardians. After hearing her plea, the board granted her a sum of money to help maintain herself and the children. A series of payments were made between December 1901 and the following July, and during that time Sian and her children were resident in the local workhouse.

The maintenance payments received by Mrs Hughes had been in the form of a loan and as William Hughes had deserted his wife, he was deemed responsible for the debt. Measures were made to recover the money, and these culminated in Hughes standing trial in August charged with desertion. He was sentenced to three months' imprisonment.

With her husband behind bars, Sian Hughes left the workhouse and, leaving the children behind, took a position as housekeeper with a recently widowed collier named Tom Maddocks who kept a cottage at Rhosrobin, a small sleepy mining hamlet on the outskirts of Wrexham. Maddocks worked as a fireman at the Rhosddu Colliery and his wife had died in the previous August, leaving him with five children, three of whom still lived at home, as did his brother.

Now Hughes was out of prison and an angry man. He discovered that his wife had found herself a home but had left the children in the workhouse. When they met and she asked him what he planned to do about the children, he told her, 'If they are still in there, let them stay there!'

In the early hours of Monday, 10th December William Hughes, who had been staying with his sister and her husband at Penycae, called at Maddocks' cottage and knocked on the door. Thinking it was Tom Maddocks returning home from working down the pit, Sian sent one of the young children, eleven year old Thomas Maddocks junior, down to open the door.

Concealing a double barrelled shotgun he had borrowed from his brother, Hughes asked the lad if his father was in. Told that he was still at work in the pit, Hughes then asked to speak to Mrs Hughes and entered the house shouting 'Sian, Sian'. Recognising his voice, she told him to sit down and wait while she got dressed.

Young Maddocks returned to bed leaving Mrs Hughes and her husband talking downstairs. A little later he was awoken by what he took to be the sound of coal being dropped on the floor. There was a second similar noise but the lad thought nothing about it and went back to sleep.

Police Constable Thomas Price Rees had had a quiet night so far on his beat when he was approached by William Hughes on the High Street, Rhosrobin. It was a little after 3.30 am. Out of breath and carrying a shotgun, Hughes spoke to the officer.

'I have been looking for one of you buggers. I have been to the police station but could not find one. I have done the devil at last. I have blown her bloody brains out.'

Rees asked Hughes if he meant what he had said, and was told: 'I have made no mistake. I levelled it at her and put them both into her, and blew her blasted guts out.' Asked whom he had shot, Hughes rambled on: 'My wife; I meant one for him and one for her.'

Hughes was taken to the police station where he repeated his confession, and as a result Constable Rees and Sergeant Harvey went to the house where they found Sian Hughes at the foot of the stairs. They arranged for the body to be removed to Wrexham mortuary where a police surgeon later confirmed that the cause of death was from gunshot wounds.

There had been no murders reported in the Denbighshire area for almost a quarter of a century and as a result the tragedy at Rhosrobin was the main topic of conversation for weeks after the event, and leading up to the trial which was held before Mr Justice Gainsford Bruce at Ruthin Assizes on 29th January 1903. Hughes pleaded not guilty to the charge of murder and his counsel offered a defence of insanity.

The basis of the prosecution's case was that the victim had been intentionally killed with a shotgun, and in his own words the prisoner had also intended to shoot Thomas Maddocks. The motive was jealousy and it was a planned assault, with Hughes taking loan of a shotgun specifically for the purpose of shooting his wife.

Proceeding vainly with a defence of insanity, Hughes' counsel tried to argue that there was no clear motive for the crime, which Hughes had committed while driven by uncontrollable rage.

Summing up the evidence, Mr Justice Bruce advised the jury that the law governing an insanity plea insists that the mental disorder must be so great as to obscure proper perception and to render a man incapable of knowing the difference between right and wrong. If that could not be proved, then he would be guilty.

The jury retired for a little under ten minutes before returning to find William Hughes guilty of wilful murder. 'Thank you, my lord,' he said as sentence of death was passed upon him.

As Hughes awaited his fate at Ruthin gaol, strenuous efforts were made on his behalf for a reprieve but, despite various petitions, including one from his former battalion, it was to no avail.

The condemned man kept a brave face while awaiting the hangman and entertained his guards on the night prior to his execution by standing on his head because, in his words: 'It will be the last time I will be able to do so!' Hughes refused to allow his aged mother to visit him after she had turned up at the prison gates with his two young children, instead penning her a farewell note. He also wrote to his brother and other relatives, saying that he hoped the Lord would be merciful to him on the other side.

The hangmen appointed were brothers William and John Billington who travelled from their home in Bolton to carry out the sentence, and at 8 am on Tuesday, 17th February 1903, William Hughes was hanged at Ruthin gaol.

It was a sad case which involved the needless loss of two lives and more tragically the orphaning of two young children left in the local workhouse by the deaths of their parents.

4

THE CHRISTMAS DAY MURDER

THE MURDER OF GWEN JONES AT HOLYHEAD, DECEMBER 1909

William Murphy was not a man to tangle with. A former soldier, he had a reputation as a hard drinking, short tempered bully who had been known to lay a man out with a single punch.

In 1907, while serving overseas, he earned a commendation for bravery when he single-handedly tackled a knife-wielding maniac. A burly soldier, overcome with sunstroke, went berserk and picking up a bayonet went on a crazed rampage, slashing out as all around people fled for their lives. Corporal Murphy sized up the situation and calmly announced he would sort it out. Ignoring warnings for his own safety, Murphy followed the soldier into a tent, emerging minutes later with the knifeman in a tight armlock. Reinforcements took the man into custody as the assembled crowd congratulated Murphy.

Several months after this incident, Murphy's unit, the Royal Anglesey Engineers Militia, was posted back to North Wales, and it was here that he first met Gwen Ellen Jones.

Gwen was 33 years old and the mother of two children, a seven year old boy and an adopted daughter of twelve named Gwladys. She was separated from her husband and earned a living as a hawker.

Murphy subsequently left the militia and took a number of jobs on Anglesey, including working on the construction of the Red Wharf Bay railway, and in the railway goods depot at Holyhead. He and Gwen set up home together and in the summer of 1909, when Murphy returned to his native Leigh in Lancashire, she accompanied him.

Murphy found work as a labourer, but as often as not spent long hours in local public houses and upon returning home drunk he would often turn violent at the slightest whim. Gwen tolerated this for several months until one particularly brutal beating left her with a black eye and split lip. She waited until Murphy fell into a drunken sleep and then gathered up her children and fled back to her parents.

25

William Murphy.

In November 1909, she left her daughter with her father in Bethesda, and taking along her young son, went to stay in a boarding house at Baker Street, Holyhead, sharing a room with a Robert Jones.

After a few weeks without Gwen, Murphy made efforts to track her down. Two weeks before Christmas, he called at her father's house and asked to see her. Her father recognised him as the man with whom his daughter had lived. He was also aware that Gwen had left him due to his violent temper, so when Murphy asked where she was he refused to tell him. Murphy then spoke to Gwladys, who let slip her mother's whereabouts.

Murphy arrived in Holyhead on 20th December and immediately began to make inquiries to find Gwen, even telling one bemused policeman: 'I'll give it to her when I find her.'

Within a few days he caught up with Gwen and asked her to come back with him. She refused and they fought. Next day she was seen sporting a large bruise and Murphy was again heard to threaten her if she did not go back with him.

On 6 pm on Christmas Day, Gwen left her home on Baker Street with Lizzie Jones, who also had a room at the boarding house, and went for a drink at the nearby Bardsey Island Inn. Inside, Murphy was at the bar drinking. He asked Gwen why she had failed to keep an earlier appointment with him, and she told him that she had turned up a little late and must have just missed him.

Later that evening Murphy asked Lizzie if she would help him arrange to see Gwen alone so he could make a plea for her to return to Leigh with him, and a short time later, his request being granted, the couple left the inn.

Within the hour Murphy walked back to the inn alone. Sporting a still bleeding scratch on his face he ordered a pint of ale, downed it in one and, bidding goodnight to some friends, he left.

He walked back to Gwen's lodgings and told one of the lodgers that he had been fighting with two men, but when Lizzie returned he admitted what he had done. 'Fetch the police,' he said quietly, 'I've killed her.'

Murphy and two lodgers from the house walked to a spot off Walthew Avenue where some houses were being built, and where a ditch had recently been excavated for a main sewage pipe. They stopped and Murphy pointed into the ditch. 'Look there, there's Gwen Ellen Jones.' Murphy then walked to the police station and confessed that he had committed a murder.

Police rushed to the scene and found Gwen lying in the ditch, the gaping wound in her throat leaving them in no doubt that she was dead. Close by they found the murder weapon. Murphy, who had been detained in custody, was then charged with murder.

In the early hours of Boxing Day, Murphy was questioned by Superintendent Prothero, the Deputy Chief Constable, and made a statement describing what had happened on the previous night. He said that after leaving the pub they had walked towards Walthew Avenue, a secluded row of residential houses that overlooked a wood.

Murphy said he pleaded with Gwen to come home but she was adamant that they were finished and again refused. In a rage, Murphy grabbed her by the throat and squeezed hard. Gwen fought vainly before he inflicted a severe wound to her throat with his knife and as the blood spurted out she collapsed in a heap. He then callously picked her up and threw her into the nearby drainage ditch. Concluding, Murphy admitted: 'We had a good hard fight and I strangled her before I cut her throat.'

His trial at Beaumaris in January 1910 was a formality. It was the first murder in Anglesey for close on 50 years and the tiny courtroom was packed solid with curious locals. Murphy could offer no reasonable defence to what the prosecution called a cold-blooded, premeditated murder. It was no surprise when the jury took less than three minutes to agree on a verdict of guilty of wilful murder. Mr Justice Pickford then donned the black cap and sentenced the prisoner to death.

On 15th February 1910, 49 year old William Murphy was hanged at Caernarfon prison: he was the last man to be executed in North Wales. He had remained calm and jovial in the condemned cell and told his guards he had no fear at the prospect of being hanged.

When hangman Harry Pierrepoint and his assistant William Willis entered the death cell the former soldier showed rare courage before his imminent death. He astonished the waiting assembly by climbing up onto a chair and jumping back down to the ground. Smiling, he turned to the startled hangmen and asked: 'I suppose it'll only be like that?'

'Yes, that's all,' Willis replied.

'Well I can do that!' he declared and walked firmly to the gallows with the same resolution he had displayed three years earlier when facing the bayonet-wielding madman.

5

THE PENYFFORDD POACHER

THE MURDER OF JOHN ROWLANDS AT PENYFFORDD, MARCH 1925

Farmhand Joseph Evans looked up from his ploughing and studied the man in the fawn raincoat who was keeping so close to the hedgerow. From his furtive manner it seemed clear that the man was a poacher. The whistle of the passing Wrexham train told Evans that it was 4.30 pm, and as he was due to finish work at five o'clock, he made a mental note to report the sighting when he finished and got back to work.

The fields of Model Farm, near Penyffordd, Flintshire were popular amongst local poachers and the south fields close to the railway track seemed to be a favoured spot.

Shortly after 5 pm, Evans detached the horses from the plough and headed back to the farmhouse, mentioning to another labourer that he thought there may be a poacher in the Upper Alps field which was bordered with the railway line. He in turn told Evans he would go and tell the boss.

Turning into the farmyard, Evans could still see the man in the raincoat in the lower corner of the field, and after stabling the horses he crossed the farmyard and saw the owner, John Jones Rowlands, walk across the stackyard and head towards the Upper Alps field. Mr Rowlands had a particular hatred of poachers and more than once in recent years he had prosecuted poachers for trespassing on his land.

In no great hurry to go home, Evans watched the owner head towards the railway line, and anxious to get a better view he walked into the garden and watched until Rowlands disappeared behind the hedges. Now unable to see either his boss or the man in the raincoat, Evans went back into the stackyard. A few minutes later he saw the mysterious figure again, and this time behaving in a strange manner, leaping around wildly. Mr Rowlands was now nowhere to be seen.

Suddenly Evans feared for his boss's safety, and went to see if he was all right. The undulating fields made it difficult to see ahead easily, dusk was beginning to fall, and as Evans hurried he saw the stranger heading towards the railway cutting. He was about to give chase when he caught sight of Rowlands lying face down on the grass close to the little stream that ran through the field.

'Mr Rowlands! Mr Rowlands! Are you all right, sir?' he called out running towards the prone figure. Reaching him, he saw that something shocking had occurred and, looking closely, he saw that Rowlands had been shot several times.

Realising Rowlands was beyond help, Evans resumed the chase of the poacher. The man had crossed the field and was climbing the fence beside the railway track when Evans next saw him. He shouted out for him to stop and as he closed in he could clearly see patches of blood on the man's fawn coat.

The man crossed the rails and climbed a fence, making off through another field towards the stile on Nant Lane. Evans followed but as he approached the stile the man seemed to reload the gun he was carrying, and fearful for his own safety, the farmhand retreated and went to summon assistance.

The local police began an investigation but soon realised that they would need specialist assistance and on the following morning they called in Scotland Yard. Whilst awaiting their arrival, Superintendent John Connah organised house to house enquiries in the local villages. Later that Friday evening, he called at a house in Penyffordd and spoke to William Theodore Brennan, a 27 year old Irishman who had recently moved to the district.

Brennan, who lived with his parents, matched the description given by Joseph Evans and was known to possess a gun and be fond of poaching. Brennan was asked to explain the scratches on his face and he claimed they were the result of a fall into some gooseberry bushes. Superintendent Connah noticed that Brennan had a fawn raincoat and that it seemed to have been washed very recently.

Asked about his movements, Brennan claimed he had not left the house at all yesterday and when his father showed the officer his small folding shotgun, Connah could tell that this was not the murder weapon. In closing, Brennan stated he did not know the location of Model Farm. It was a costly slip.

On the following afternoon Chief Inspector Cornish and Detective Sergeant Mallet arrived from Scotland Yard to take over the hunt for the killer. They spent the following day going over the available evidence and it was when Chief Inspector Cornish re-read Brennan's statement that he noticed something that did not ring true.

Chief Inspector Cornish had already compiled a list of all local poachers who were known to have used the fields around Model Farm and one name on this list was William Brennan. The Scotland Yard men re-visited Brennan and he was asked to go over his statement again. The second statement mirrored the first and Brennan was adamant he was nowhere near the farm on Thursday.

A check on his fawn raincoat yielded no further clues, there were no noticeable signs of blood, although it had clearly been washed recently. Also, Brennan's gun was closely examined and it was evidently not the type used to kill Mr Rowlands.

Nevertheless, Cornish felt he was hiding something and asked Brennan to accompany them back to Caergwrle police station for further questions. Brennan was asked if he would take part in an identity parade which was being organised at Mold and he agreed.

Nine men of similar height and build formed a line and Joseph Evans and a neighbouring farmer, Mr Reynolds, who had also seen the mystery man on the Thursday afternoon, were invited to take part. Neither picked out Brennan, although the man Evans indicated bore him a strong resemblance.

Cornish was still convinced that he had his man, but even he admitted to being a little surprised when he received word that Brennan wished to speak to him. Brennan was cautioned before he launched into a full confession, in which he claimed everything he had told the officers up to now was untrue.

He admitted owning another shotgun, a single breech twelve bore – the type used to kill Mr Rowlands – which broke down into small pieces to be carried in the inside pocket of his raincoat.

Brennan stated that on the Thursday afternoon he was shooting rabbits in the field when Rowlands grabbed him. Despite his promise to surrender the rabbits he had shot if he was released, Rowlands refused and insisted Brennan hand over his gun. He said the two men struggled and the gun went off accidentally, felling the farm owner. In a panic Brennan then reloaded and fired again to make good his escape. It was at this point that he saw Evans approach and give chase.

Brennan said that when he saw Evans turn back, he took off his coat and turned it inside out and he then hid the gun in a ditch. He successfully covered his traces so his family suspected nothing, and after supper when his parents retired for the night, he crept downstairs and finished cleaning up his shoes and coat.

On the following day he took officers into the field and showed them where he had hidden the shotgun. 'This is my gun, the one I did the shooting with,' he said to the officers, handing the pieces over.

In June of that year William Brennan stood trial at Mold Assizes. Based on the detailed confession he had made to police, his counsel took the only option open to them and pleaded insanity. 'In shooting

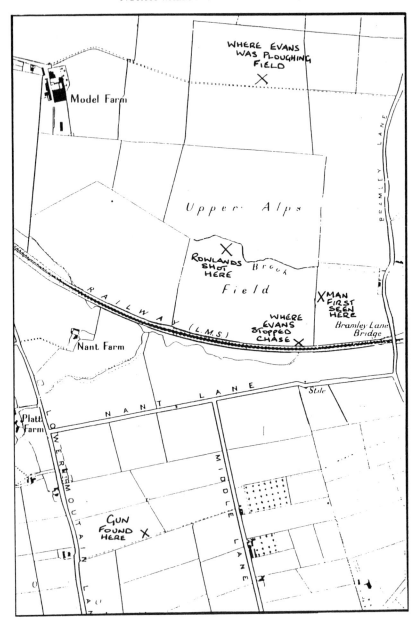

Map of the fields around Model Farm.

Mr Rowlands,' his counsel stated, 'he had reacted like a wild animal, his one instinct to destroy the enemy. There is no doubt he would have acted in an exactly similar way if a policeman had been present at the time of the shooting.'

It was only a short trial and after considering their verdict, the jury came down on the side of the defence and found the prisoner guilty but insane. The judge ordered that Brennan be sent to Broadmoor Criminal Lunatic Asylum where he died some years later.

6

A FAMILY TRAGEDY

THE MURDER OF WILLIAM WILLIAMS AT LLANRWST,
DECEMBER 1937

Forty eight year old Caroline Williams lived with her husband William, a partly crippled former collier turned hawker, 20 years her senior, in a squalid house on Scotland Street, Llanrwst, Denbighshire. They shared their home, which had neither running water nor lighting and was described in court as little more than a hovel, with the youngest of their seven children, whilst the eldest son George had a house that stood back to back with his parents' home.

On Christmas Day 1937, Caroline and her husband returned home after spending the lunchtime drinking in a local pub. At 2.30 pm, they were seen by two of their sons, George and Henry, in their living room. Both had had a lot to drink, in particular their father, who was clearly quite drunk, and he sat by the fire singing carols as his wife played the accordion.

The sons left the room and went on to George's house. At 4 pm, William Williams, who because of his disability made a distinctive sound when he walked, was heard by a neighbour walking to the outside water tap. A few minutes later this same neighbour saw Mrs Williams standing at her window. He thought she looked upset.

A short time later, Mrs Williams hurried to her son's house and cried: 'Come at once. Something has happened to your father!' George followed her back and found his father with a wound to his neck. 'I am all right, son,' he said, closing his eyes. George rushed to fetch the local doctor but by the time help arrived it was too late, and William Williams was dead.

The body was removed for examination by police surgeon Dr Donald Currie, who travelled down from Colwyn Bay. The doctor was of the opinion that the wound to Mr Williams' neck could not have been self inflicted, and the probable weapon used was a large kitchen knife which had been found 'thick with blood' in the kitchen area.

When detectives questioned Mrs Williams about the assault she immediately launched into a fierce condemnation of her brother-in-law, Robert Lovell, and claimed: 'This is the result of the Christmas beer.' She then gave out a tirade of foul and abusive language, all the while claiming that Lovell had stabbed her husband. When asked why he should have done so, she said that he had been jealous of Mr Williams for a long time and had lost his temper while drunk.

The Chief Constable of Denbighshire took over the investigation and began by detaining Lovell for further questioning. While he was being held in custody, and investigations into his movements on Christmas Day afternoon were made, Mrs Williams was further questioned and made several statements.

Four days after the stabbing, she was charged with the murder of her husband and remanded in custody. Robert Lovell was released without charge.

Mrs Williams stood trial for the murder of her husband at Denbighshire Winter Assizes, held at Ruthin Castle on Friday, 4th February 1938, before Mr Justice Atkinson. She was defended by Mr Temple Morris KC and Mr Emlyn Jones, whilst Mr Ralph Sutton KC and Mr J.F. Marnum appeared for the Crown. She pleaded not guilty to the charge of murder.

The court was told that Mrs Williams habitually carried a carving knife, which she had claimed was for protection against her husband, who could turn violent when drunk. The prosecution stated that the fatal blow had been delivered whilst the victim was seated in his armchair and this discounted any claim that the blow was made in self-defence or had been self inflicted.

Whilst being questioned prior to her arrest, Mrs Williams had made a number of statements about the events of that fateful day and after first saying that her husband had fallen against the fender while holding a knife, she later claimed that Robert Lovell, the husband of her sister Emily, had stabbed William Williams following a jealous quarrel. It was in her final statement, made a few days later, that she claimed her husband had committed suicide by stabbing himself in the neck.

Emily Lovell was called to the stand and said that on more than one occasion she had called at her sister's house in the midst of a quarrel, and on the last occasion Caroline Williams had been found standing over her husband brandishing the knife and threatening: 'I'll have you yet, you old hypocrite!' Mrs Lovell claimed she had disarmed her sister and warned: 'Caroline, you'll use that knife once too often you know.'

Caroline Williams' defence was that her husband had committed suicide and on the advice of her counsel she declined to go into the witness box. For the defence, Mr Temple Morris said that it would be idle for him to contend that the finger of suspicion was not pointed at the accused, but he submitted that his client was not guilty of murder.

As the judge finished his summing up, he told the jury that in some instances it was possible for them to find that the proved facts did not establish murder, but established manslaughter. He did not think it was possible in this case.

They needed just 25 minutes to find Caroline Williams guilty as charged and the short trial ended with Mr Justice Atkinson passing sentence of death upon the prisoner. The jury added a strong recommendation for mercy.

Her counsel immediately lodged notice of appeal, based on the judge's misdirection and non-direction of the jury on a number of issues, and this was heard before the Lord Chief Justice, Mr Justice Charles, and Mr Justice Goddard at the Court of Criminal Appeal on 1st March 1938.

The appeal judges dismissed the appeal and stated that the judge's summing up was in no way open to criticism. Mrs Williams was returned to the condemned cell at Manchester prison where on the following morning she received news that her life had been spared and she would instead face a life in prison.

Life imprisonment in this case was a little over twelve months; Mrs Williams walked free shortly after the outbreak of the Second World War.

7

AS OLD AS HUMANITY

THE MURDER OF MARGARET DAVIES AT COEDPOETH,
MAY 1938

The stranger finished his cigarette and crushed the butt under his foot. It was 7 pm on Monday, 2nd May 1938, and Bill Davies and John Harrison were talking outside their homes at Mount Zion, Top Brymbo, on the outskirts of Wrexham. For the last ten minutes the stranger had been leaning against the gate at the mill lodge at Brymbo Pool staring into space and something about his manner held their attention. Now they watched in amazement as the man suddenly climbed over the small fence and, shedding first his hat, then his overcoat, approached the pool.

His intentions quickly became apparent and after calling out for another neighbour to fetch the police the two men hurried across the road. It was a only a short distance, but by the time they reached the banking the man was already submerged in the murky depths.

Davies and Harrison edged themselves in, attempting to pull the man clear, and as they did so he fought and struggled. 'Let me go, please,' he begged, as much against his will he was dragged to safety. A third man, Tom Bellis, had by this time joined the rescuers, carrying a coil of rope intended as a lifeline. The rope was now utilised to shackle him as he fought grimly for his freedom.

Now unable to do himself or his rescuers any harm, the man was taken to Wrexham hospital where he was treated for concussion. He stubbornly refused to reveal his identity and a policeman was called to speak to him. Fortunately, the officer did not have far to travel, for already at the hospital were a number of policemen investigating the brutal assault on a Coedpoeth landlady earlier that afternoon, and whose condition had deteriorated to the extent that she was not expected to last the night.

Forty eight year old Margaret Davies lived at 63, Talwrn Road, Coedpoeth, with her second husband Thomas Bertram 'Bert' Davies, and her son from her first marriage, Dennis Charles Clowes. Mrs

Davies was a wealthy woman; not only did she own her own spacious home at Coedpoeth, which she ran as a boarding house, but she also had a tidy sum in the bank. Despite his wife's reported wealth, Davies earned his own living as a bricklayer, as did her son. Relations between husband and wife appeared not to be good and they slept in separate rooms, she having a room to herself while he shared a room with his stepson.

It was her husband and son who had found her battered body when they returned home from work at 5.40 pm. Unable to gain entry the two men walked to the rear of the house, where they found the spare key was missing. They noticed nothing amiss. Thinking his wife had popped out, Bert Davies waited outside while his son walked down to the road to see if he could find his mother.

Returning a short time later, Dennis Clowes found his stepfather still waiting outside. This time they peered through the sitting room window whereupon they could make out the body of Mrs Davies on the floor. As Dennis went to fetch the local doctor, Davies climbed through another downstairs window, but when he tried to open the sitting room door he found it locked. Picking up a poker from the grate he forced the lock.

Returning with the son, Dr David Evans found that Mrs Davies had severe wounds to her head, presumably caused by the bloodstained hammer that lay in the grate, and he wasted no time in getting her transferred to the Wrexham hospital. She died from her wounds later that night.

Detectives called to investigate the vicious assault soon had a prime suspect. Missing from his room at the house on Talwrn Road was the lodger Frank Booth Joynson, a 45 year old Stockport bookmaker who carried out his business from a shop at Brymbo. Once word had reached them about the strange suicide attempt at Brymbo, officers visited the man's bedside where he later admitted that his name was Frank Joynson.

Linking Joynson to the murder was simple. Inside Mrs Davies' bedroom were close on 150 letters, each written by Joynson, in which he declared his love for 'his Madge'. Dating back many months, and with postmarks from across the country they charted what appeared to be a crusade of almost certainly unrequited love, with passages such as 'Don't drop me like that. . . I know in my heart you don't mean it.'

Reading through the large bundle of letters, detectives formed a picture of the events that had led to Madge Davies receiving her fatal wounds. It seemed that Joynson had taken a room with the Davieses in 1937 and there appeared to have been a brief romance between him and Mrs Davies. However, this relationship was clearly long over, as the majority of his letters pleaded for her to reconsider.

It also seemed clear that Joynson was jealous of a man named Fred

Brymbo Pool.

Chesworth he suspected was having an affair with Mrs Davies. Some of the more recent letters were addressed to Bert Davies, and apparently had been intercepted by Madge, in which he warned Davies about his wife's infidelity.

More conclusive proof that Joynson had killed Mrs Davies was supplied by several notes Joynson had left prior to his failed suicide attempt at Brymbo Pool. One such note found beside the body read:

'Bert,

I have done this, no one else, and the cause of it is Chesworth from Nant Farm, your biggest enemy. He was planning with her to run away together. He hates the sight of you. We are madly in love now and always have been. She has been mother, wife and everything to me. Other chaps come into her life but no other man shall have anything to do with her but me.

She has about £15,000 in the bank and you were not going to see a penny of it, nor were the kids. Chesworth was going to benefit from that, inducing her to take a farm at Dorset and live with him. I have put a stop to that. . .

. . . It has to be the end. I have murdered an angel. She has gone and I am going with her. If I damn well cannot have her to myself in this world I will rot in hell.'

A check on Joynson's movements earlier on the day of the murder found that he had left the house on Talwrn Road shortly before dinner and had spent the best part of the afternoon in a number of pubs in and around Brymbo. One witness told police that he had spoken to Joynson at 1 pm and he was drunk. Asked how he had managed to get in such a state at this hour, Joynson had told the man that he had a bottle of whisky back at the shop.

Officers later called at the shop at Lodge, Brymbo, and found further clues, including the missing key from Talwrn Road. Several notes had been left there by Joynson, addressed to various people, including the coroner.

One brief note was addressed to the Wrexham Gas Company. It seemed to have been written in a fit of pique after a failed suicide attempt: a pipe was lying on a pillow, evidence that Joynson had tried to gas himself. The note was short and to the point: 'Your bloody gas is no good!'

Subsequently, Frank Booth Joynson stood trial before Mr Justice Singleton at Ruthin Assizes. Prosecuting counsel, Mr Stable KC, said that Mrs Davies appeared to have occupied his thoughts to the exclusion of all else. Describing it as a crime as old as humanity, Mr Stable said proof of Joynson's guilt was supplied by his own hand and he had killed the woman he loved, unable to face up to the fact that she could not or would not return his affections.

In his defence, Mr Ralph Sutton KC pleaded that Joynson was suffering from what he termed *petit mal* – a form of minor epilepsy. Combined with his mixed emotions, this caused him to become unstable of mind. He called medical evidence to support this theory and said further proof was that the prisoner had made no attempt to conceal his guilt after committing the crime.

The jury needed just 20 minutes to find Joynson guilty of wilful murder and he became the second resident of North Wales to be sentenced to death in 1938.

An appeal was launched on his behalf but was quickly rejected and he was returned to the death cell at Shrewsbury. Although many men had occupied this same cell at Shrewsbury prison, the hangman had been an infrequent visitor in recent times and there had not been a hanging here for over 15 years.

For a time it seemed that Joynson would end this trend and preparations were well under way before it was announced that, like Mrs Williams a few months earlier, he had been granted a reprieve.

Spared the rope, Frank Booth Joynson was sentenced to life imprisonment for the murder of the woman he loved. Ten years almost to the day, he walked free from prison and set about rebuilding his shattered life.

8

A DOCTOR'S OBSESSION

THE MURDER OF JOAN REAY AND JOHN HADEN AT CONWY, AUGUST 1942

On a warm Thursday night, 27th August 1942, the old fashioned darts room at the Groes Hotel, Groesynyd, near Conwy, was playing host to a lively crowd. A pianist entertained whilst others enjoyed a game of darts and a pleasant drink and chat. Suddenly, and without warning, the heavy blackout drapes were pushed aside and the twin barrels of a shotgun were thrust through the partially opened window.

Two shots rang out in quick succession before the gun was immediately withdrawn. John Haden, a 30 year old leather goods manufacturer of Aldridge, Staffordshire, who had been standing with his back to the window, facing the dartboard, was hit in the back with the first shot and he fell to the floor dead.

The second shot struck Mrs Joan Reay, the 27 year old wife of a Llandudno doctor. She cried out in pain as she was hit in the abdomen, slumping to the ground mortally wounded. Mrs Haden and several other guests ran outside in search of her husband's killer but the assailant was nowhere to be seen.

A telephone call was made to the local police station and Sergeant Ederyn Jones and a police constable rushed to the hotel. Other officers, aided by special constables and soldiers, began a search for the killer. An ambulance took Mrs Reay to the hospital at Llandudno where she died later that night.

As the Chief Constable of Caernarfonshire, Mr Pritchard, arrived at the hotel accompanied by the Home Office appointed pathologist, Dr James Firth from Preston, it was learned that Mrs Reay's estranged husband Dr John Reay had been seen in the grounds of the hotel on two separate occasions earlier that afternoon. The Reays had been separated for over twelve months and an officer was sent to Llandudno to

A wedding day photograph of Dr and Mrs Reay.

question the doctor. He reported that Dr Reay was not at home and a search was begun for him.

Forty year old Dr Reay was a well respected practitioner with a thriving surgery at Rindleford, Queens Road, Llandudno. He had married Joan Parry in 1934. She was his second wife, his first wife having died two years earlier leaving him with a young daughter, Joyce. He was a native of South Shields and had been practising in Llandudno for the past twelve years having graduated from King's College, Newcastle-upon-Tyne. Coincidentally, one of his tutors at the college was the same Dr Firth called in to assist the police in their investigations.

The search for Dr Reay ended in the early hours of the following morning when Conwy postman David Jones found his small blue car parked in a little-used mountainside quarry at Tanybwich, near the Sychnant Pass.

Officers hurried to the scene to find the doctor unconscious in the driving seat of the car. On the passenger seat were a number of bottles of pills and on the back seat was a double barrelled shotgun. Dr Reay was removed to Llandudno hospital where officers stood guard at his bedside while efforts were made to revive him.

Detectives spoke to Mrs Camwen Jones, Dr Reay's housekeeper of four years, and she told them that the relationship between the couple had deteriorated in recent years and that when his wife left him in July

1941, going to stay with Mrs Haden and her husband in Staffordshire, he became withdrawn and very quiet.

Describing the events of the day of Mrs Reay's murder, Mrs Jones told police that it had been Dr Reay's half day at the surgery and that after seeing his daughter he had changed into his tennis clothes and gone out. Besides being a keen tennis player, the doctor was also fond of shooting game and kept two shotguns.

Mrs Jones said that she had arrived at the surgery on Friday morning unaware of the events of the previous night, but she had found a note addressed to her amongst a bundle of letters and after reading it she called the police.

Having firmly established a link between both victims and Dr Reay, the next step was to prove beyond doubt that it was the doctor who had fired the shots and to try to find a motive for the killings.

The condition of the doctor remained critical as officers learned of events that took place outside the Groes Hotel on the Thursday afternoon. A distraught Mrs Haden told police that the doctor had approached Mrs Reay and asked her if she was still going ahead with the planned divorce.

Mrs Reay had related this conversation to Mrs Haden later that evening and Mrs Haden had formed the impression that not only was the doctor upset that his wife would not return to him, but was also concerned that the ensuing scandal could be enough to drive him from the town.

Mrs Haden was present later that evening when she overheard the doctor in conversation with her husband, the gist of which seemed to be that Dr Reay believed that John Haden was having an affair with his wife. There was no evidence to support this claim and Mrs Haden strenuously denied it. Reay had finished this short confrontation with the threat: 'Two of you have a sticky time coming.'

Mrs Haden concluded her statement by saying that at 10.30 pm, Thursday night, she had looked out of the hotel window and spotted Dr Reay sitting on a bench in the grounds.

John Reay never regained consciousness and died shortly after noon on the following Sunday. A post-mortem ascertained the cause of death to be heart failure due to bronchial pneumonia and toxic myocarditis: the result of an overdose of barbiturate tablets.

A month after the tragedy an inquest was held at Llandudno where the known facts were presented to a coroner's jury. Evidence was given that supported the theory that Dr John Reay had shot dead his wife and a man he believed, without the slightest piece of evidence, to be having an affair with her. Having committed the double killing, he then drove to a deserted quarry and took an overdose of tablets, which brought about his own death a little over 48 hours later.

Evidence was heard from Dr Reay's own doctor and the Royal Navy medical officer who had examined Reay when he had taken a medical examination prior to his enlistment as a surgeon lieutenant in the previous autumn, and both stated that he showed marked signs of mental instability.

After being directed by the coroner on certain legal points, the jury retired for 20 minutes before announcing their verdict. In the cases of Joan Reay and John Haden, the verdict was one of murder against John Reay, and in the case of John Reay the verdict was felo-de-se (suicide).

It is not clear from reading what little was reported on the case in the thin wartime newspapers when Dr Reay first assumed that John Haden was having an affair with his wife. It is hard to believe, and indeed very unlikely, that Mrs Haden would have invited her husband's mistress into the house. Prior to the murder Reay had made plans to take out a summons against John Haden on a charge of enticing his wife away from home. A solicitor later looked over the case and declared the summons would have had absolutely no chance of succeeding.

Obsessed and unhappy, Dr Reay was driven into committing a terrible crime after relentlessly torturing himself that his estranged wife was unfaithful.

9

BREAKING THE COMMANDMENTS

THE MANSLAUGHTER OF IVY NETTLETON AT RED WHARF BAY, OCTOBER 1945

There was a curious coincidence concerning the tragedy that took place at peaceful Red Wharf Bay in the weeks following the end of the Second World War. Strangely, not only did both the victim and her killer originate from Manchester, over 100 miles away, but the house where the crime took place was owned by a Mancunian and it was a Manchester woman who started the murder hunt.

Staff nurse Sheila Holt was enjoying a well earned break from her duties at Manchester's busy Ancoats Hospital and, along with her mother and sister Pamela, was making the most of the mild weather in the first peacetime autumn for six years. Deciding on a short holiday by the sea, the family had rented a bungalow at Benllech, Anglesey.

On Wednesday afternoon, 24th October 1945, Sheila and Pamela went horse riding and after passing through the local village and country lanes they approached Red Wharf Bay. Galloping across the almost deserted sands, Sheila spotted what appeared to be a body half buried in the sand. Climbing off the horse, she found her fears were justified and the sisters hurried back to Benllech to fetch a policeman.

Police Constable William Roberts accompanied the girls back to the beach. The body appeared to be that of a middle-aged woman, lying with her head, which was covered with a pillow-case, facing towards Castle Rock and her feet pointing out to sea. She had a stocking tied around her neck, knotted at the back. Removing the pillow-case he found that cotton wool in the form of a pad had been placed over the face, which bore the traces of a fearful beating, and underneath this a tea towel was tied with a reef knot around the throat.

It was clear from the outset she was the victim of foul play and it was only a matter of time before the Chief Constable, Mr Prothero, called in Scotland Yard. Detective Inspector McDonald and Detective Sergeant Hannam journeyed up to Anglesey hotly pursued by a large posse of press reporters from Fleet Street, who sensed a major murder case was about to break.

There had been two world wars since the last murder case on Anglesey and as a result local interest in the discovery of the body was at fever pitch. Cashing in on the gruesome tourist attraction, more than one enterprising coach operator ferried curious sightseers from miles around to watch police officers, using a plough borrowed from a neighbouring farmer, dig up the beach to check that other bodies were not buried beneath the sands.

The story was reported in most of the the national dailies and picked up on by many regional evening papers, one of which was read by Mrs Sarah Walker who lived with her husband at Stalybridge in Cheshire.

The Walkers had been to Red Wharf Bay only a few weeks earlier, staying with their daughter Ivy and her husband Arthur Nettleton, in a rented cottage overlooking the bay. She had last seen Ivy on 3rd October when they left her and Arthur to finish their holiday alone.

Since that time 32 year old Arthur Nettleton had written Sarah a lengthy letter saying Ivy was unwell and was staying in bed for a couple of days. On 19th October he called at the Walkers' house and said that they had finished their holiday on the previous Saturday, and that since then Ivy had left him, refusing to say where she was going. Although Sarah knew her daughter to be somewhat neurotic and not in the best of health, Nettleton was a little too glib with his account of what had happened and this worried her.

When the story of the discovery of a body at Red Wharf Bay broke, Sarah Walker rushed round to see Nettleton. He assured her that it could not be Ivy as he had seen her a few days earlier when she had called to collect some clothes from the house. Again she would not tell him where she was staying but he thought it was somewhere in Manchester.

On the following day Sarah Walker again spoke to her son-in-law, and again Nettleton tried to reassure her, this time saying that Ivy was staying in a shelter at the Midland Hotel, Manchester. Undeterred, later that afternoon Sarah Walker called into her local police station and voiced her suspicions.

Next morning Nettleton responded to a police appeal asking for previous occupants at Royd Cottage, the bayside holiday home, to come forward. He reported to the front desk at Stalybridge police station and told the sergeant that he and his wife had stayed at Red Wharf Bay early in October.

He was interviewed by Inspector Cook and gave him an account of his movements since leaving Red Wharf Bay. He told the officer that his wife had left him while they were at Red Wharf Bay and he had travelled to Rhyl where he thought she might have gone. He said he had last seen his wife on Thursday 18th October and that he had not seen her since then. He had read about the body found at Red Wharf Bay but it could not be Ivy as the description was of a woman much taller than his wife.

By coincidence, Inspector Cook had been on duty on the previous day when Mrs Walker had reported her suspicions to the police and after weighing up the few facts he telephoned Inspector McDonald at the murder headquarters. As a result the two Scotland Yard officers caught the next train, arriving at Stalybridge police station later that evening. Both went to see Nettleton and he told them a similar tale to the one he had furnished Inspector Cook with several hours earlier.

The presence of the Scotland Yard officers seemed to have shaken Nettleton and as he finished the statement, Inspector McDonald left him alone with his thoughts. A few minutes later McDonald returned and Nettleton spoke to him again: 'Sir, I want the thing straight. All I have said is lies. I did it.' He then made a further statement admitting his guilt:

'On the morning of October 8th I got up early and took my wife's breakfast to her in bed. Then I went into the kitchen to iron my shirt. My wife began shouting from the bedroom about my going to the Health Office about the chance of getting a nearby cottage. I lost my temper and when my wife came into the kitchen I swung round and hit her full in the face with the hot iron. She had a bread-knife in her hand which I had not seen before. I grabbed it from her and I cannot tell you how many times I hit her after that.' He then broke down and was in tears as a charge of wilful murder was read to him.

Arthur Albert Nettleton stood trial before Mr Justice Stable at Beaumaris Assizes on 21st January 1946. Despite the cold weather, queues formed in the early hours to see a man stand trial for his life.

Mr Edmund Davies KC led for the defence, and as the prosecution had built its case mainly around the confession Nettleton had made at Stalybridge, Davies knew that realistically there were only two possible verdicts: guilty of murder or guilty of manslaughter. They set about in earnest trying to secure the latter.

Their evidence was based around a bizarre document which Davies said resembled the Biblical Commandments. Before drawing the court's attention to it he asked Nettleton if he loved his wife. Nettleton sobbed, 'I loved my wife. I always loved her.'

He went on to describe how Nettleton had met his wife in 1937 and they had married two years later. From the start Ivy Nettleton was a jealous woman, so much so that she resented her husband joining the army as part of his duties was in the hospital where he came into contact with many female nurses.

Fearing that he would be called overseas once war broke out, she wrote out a document which was headed 'Solemn Promise'. It read: 'This is a solemn promise that I shall always be faithful to my darling Ivy, and I promise to love, honour and obey all her wishes in sickness and health. I promise to make her as happy as is humanly possible and keep her in the best possible way I can afford. I promise I shall love her more than anything or anybody in creation has ever been loved. I only ask God to spare me for many years so that I will be able to carry out these promises.'

When he returned from overseas service she became obsessed that he had had a good time in Italy, in her words: 'Sucking oranges, going to ENSA concerts and dancing in Naples.'

Although it was clear to both her husband and her family that Ivy was suffering from a mental illness, her doctor diagnosed that she was psycho-neurotic, unstable and hysterical, but not a case for certification as of unsound mind. In other words she was a borderline case, and the only person who had to cope with her mood swings and hysteria was her down-trodden, loving husband.

So eager was Nettleton to keep the peace with his wife that he put his name on the end of a document his wife drafted and which his counsel had earlier referred to as 'The Commandments'. The 17 points were read out in court:

1. There shall be but one woman, my wife Ivy.
2. That her wishes and plans shall be mine also.
3. The decision of my wife Ivy in all matters shall be the right as well as the final one.
4. Never will I speak to or have anything to do with women, unless to answer them when it is absolutely necessary.
5. Never will I make new friends or contact old ones without the consent and approval of my wife Ivy.
6. Never will I go against any of my wife's dreams, schemes, plans, wishes or ideals.
7. Her ideals, her feelings, shall be respected by me always.
8. The hatreds of my wife shall be mine also.
9. Never will I wear a uniform after this war.
10. Never will I do anything to the benefit of man or country but only for the personal benefit of my wife and myself.
11. Never will I be a soldier except in appearance. Always for myself and my wife I will take, but never give.
12. I will live, work and play for one person only, my wife Ivy.
13. I will seek not, or write, or contact in any way, any of my relatives without consent of my wife, Ivy.
14. I will not lie to or cheat my wife. May God strike me dead if ever again I do.

15. Never will I speak of my adventures overseas in the presence of my wife unless she approves.
16. Never will I write to anyone or have dealing with anyone without the permission of my wife.
17. Should I ever see Mr Eyre [a sergeant who had introduced Nettleton to the Territorial Army before the war] I do solemnly swear to spit in his eye whatever the time or place.

The document ended with the atonement: 'I will repay my wife in love and kindness for getting me back to England, in great pain and suffering to herself.'

The defence asked the jury to consider that Nettleton had killed his wife under a great deal of mental stress and that in no way could it be shown that the crime was premeditated. Forensic evidence taken from the body and from items found at the bungalow suggested that Nettleton's version of events as described to the police at Stalybridge was consistent with the truth.

The prosecution suggested to the accused that he had planned to kill his wife as he had tired of her incessant nagging. Mr Glyn-Jones KC, for the prosecution, told the court that sympathy for the man should not cloud the issue that he had committed a brutal murder.

After the judge had summed up the evidence the jury of nine men and three women pondered their verdict for several hours before returning to find the prisoner not guilty of murder, but guilty of manslaughter.

Mr Justice Stable told Nettleton that the jury had taken a merciful view of the incident, and it was one with which he agreed. 'I have no doubt that during the last twelve months of your wife's life, your life was absolutely intolerable. Nevertheless you could have left her . . . Women, however tiresome, must be protected and the law cannot possibly permit or condone conduct of this kind.'

He then sentenced Nettleton to five years' imprisonment. In contrast to the baying mob who had called for his blood when Nettleton was brought back to Anglesey to stand trial, there were cheers from the packed gallery as the verdict was announced and several people tried to shake his hand before he was ushered to the cells below.

10

ANOTHER MAN'S CHILD

THE MURDER OF GWENDOLINE JONES AT BETHEL, ANGLESEY,
MAY 1947

Just before the end of the Second World War, Gwendoline Jones, a 22 year old domestic servant, met and fell in love with Owen Thomas Richards, a 21 year old farm labourer from Rhostrehwfa, Llangefni. A year later they began a more intimate relationship.

In February 1947, Gwen left Richards and went to live at Penygroes, Trefdraeth, with another man, a John Williams. Her feelings for Richards were not so easily dismissed however, and when she found she was pregnant she contacted him. Over the next few months letters passed between them, but despite Gwen's insistence that the baby was his, Richards was having none of it, and demanded that she have a blood test so that he could prove he was not the father of the child.

Then early on the morning of Thursday, 22nd May 1947, Gwen Jones was found dead. Farmer William Hughes, of Bodorgan, Anglesey, was tending to his land when he approached Ty'n Sarn field, near Bethel, and spotted a figure lying in the hedgerow. Taking a closer look, he saw the body of a young woman lying face down. He called the police and they in turn summoned pathologist Dr Grace.

Examining the body, police found that she had been shot twice in the head. It appeared that a shotgun had been fired from a matter of inches away; the first shot had blown her brains out, and she had been dead before the second round was discharged.

Enquiries into Gwen's background soon led the police to the home of Owen Richards at Rhostrehwfa. They spoke to Richards' parents and asked to see their son's shotgun and the clothing he had worn on the previous night. His parents handed over just the shotgun, which they noticed had been sawn down, adding that he must still be wearing the clothes worn yesterday. Detectives then set out to interview Richards, who was at work on Bodwina Farm.

Gwendoline Jones.

Arriving later that afternoon, and led by Superintendent Jones, they questioned Richards. 'We have seen the body of Gwen Jones and are making enquiries into her death. Where were you last night?' Richards denied being anywhere near where the body was found on the previous evening. Assuming the interview was over, he walked back with the officers to their car where he spotted his shotgun on the back seat.

'Why have you got that?' he asked, clearly taken aback.

'It is to be sent for forensic examination,' he was told.

Richards then sighed heavily and made a fresh statement in which he admitted meeting his former lover the previous evening. She was wrongly blaming him for her condition. 'I have my future to think of, you know,' he said, close to tears. Asked what he had done with the cartridges, Richards said that he had fired two at Gwen and the rest were back at home.

The officers accompanied Richards back to Rhostrehwfa, where he climbed into his loft and handed them the clothes he had worn on the previous night. A search of the house also found the recently sawn off shotgun barrel.

Richards was then taken to the local police station where he made a statement in Welsh. He said that after hearing that Gwen was saying he was the father of her child he had received a letter from Gwen asking him to meet her. They met briefly on 13th May, when she told him she was refusing to have the blood test he had asked her to take. He then said that he arranged to meet her again: 'I had made up my mind that if she wouldn't have the blood test, I would [pausing] – well, you know what I mean.'

Asked what had happened on the previous night, Richards told the officers that they had met up and had walked into the field together. They argued over her refusal to take the test and in a rage, 'I lost my temper a bit and shot her. I do not know where. I left her there, and took the gun home and cleaned it,' he concluded.

Richards was remanded in custody while detectives checked out the statement. A search of the house at Penygroes found seven letters addressed to Gwen Jones, each written by Owen Richards. In one letter he apologised for not behaving properly with her, whilst in another he apologised for failing to meet her as arranged. They were clearly still involved with each other. She had written to him that month saying that she loved him and inviting him to the house. On 16th May, however, he had written to Gwen saying that he had been told certain things about her and as a result he no longer wanted to see her again. The letter also stated that he was not the father of her baby, and for her to leave him alone as he hoped to marry a girl from Llandudno.

It was found that on the day of the murder, Richards had finished work at 7 pm and gone home, where he had sawn off the barrel of the shotgun. His brother had witnessed this. Meanwhile, in Penygroes, John Williams had left his house at 8 pm and shortly afterwards a neighbour saw Gwen Jones leave.

Several local witnesses told police that they had heard two shots at 11.15 pm. This was not an unusual occurrence as poachers frequented the area after dark. However, at 11.25 pm, three men saw a man identified as Richards cycling away from Ty'n Sarn field towards Bodwina Farm.

Richards had to wait five months before his case came to trial at Caernarfon Assizes in October, presided over by Mr Justice Stable.

Mr Athrian Davies KC, acting for the defence, submitted that the shooting was an accident and described how Richards had recently been asked by an uncle to shoot a rabbit for him. Whilst cycling, he had fallen from the bicycle and had damaged the gun barrel to such an extent that he was forced to saw it down. The fall had also damaged the firing mechanism which now fired at the slightest touch. Mr Davies called Sergeant Allen of the Preston forensic laboratory who had examined the gun and he concurred with this latter claim.

After meeting Gwen in the field, Richards claimed they began to quarrel, whereupon she struck him and he retaliated, and during the scuffle the gun was accidentally discharged. Regarding the second shot, Mr Davies said: 'It may be that the quite misguided idea of putting an injured person out of her misery crossed his mind.'

Mr Davies also went to lengths to describe various accidents that his client had suffered in the past. Richards suffered a great deal from headaches, the result of an accident at work in 1938 when a pitchfork became embedded in his left temple. Prompt action saved his life but he was to be blighted with head pains from then on. In 1946 he was involved in another accident when the tractor he was driving overturned in the field. He received another blow to the head and the headaches became worse. In fact, they were so severe as to render him temporarily insane at times.

Mr Glyn-Jones KC, leading for the Crown, dismissed the defence's plea by claiming that Richards' story was pure invention. He had intentionally shot Gwen Jones because she had become a nuisance to him.

'You shot her like a dog, didn't you?' he asked coldly.

'No, sir,' Richards replied.

Mr Glyn Jones also pointed out that forensic evidence had suggested that the fatal shots had been fired in a downward direction, more in line with the gun being pointed deliberately at someone lying on the ground, than of someone struggling, in which case they might reasonably expect the trajectory of the bullet to be upward.

Telephone No ....

All communications should be addressed
to " The Governor " (not to any Official
by name) and the following number
quoted. ....

H. M. Prison,
LIVERPOOL

18th November, 1947

Your ref ....

Dear Sir,

<u>2532 Owen Thomas RICHARDS</u>

Further to our previous communications, I have now
to inform you that the above named prisoner's appeal was
dismissed yesterday and the execution has therefore been
fixed for 9.0 a.m. on Tuesday, December 2nd, 1947.

I enclose herewith the necessary railway warrant
for your use on Monday, December 1st, and I shall be glad
if you will confirm receipt and that you will be present
to carry out the execution.

Yours faithfully

Governor.

Letter advising the hangman of the revised date of Owen Richards' execution.
He was reprieved 48 hours before the scheduled date.

Once both the prosecution and defence had finished giving their
evidence, Mr Justice Stable began his summing up. Although the
defence had sought to show that Richards could be suffering from a
form of insanity, the judge quickly dismissed this by saying that a
verdict of 'murder but insane' could not be brought on this case. He
also told the jury there was no evidence to support a verdict of
manslaughter; the only possible verdicts they could reach on the
evidence heard in the court were guilty of murder or not guilty.

Retiring for a little over two hours, the jury returned to find the
prisoner guilty of murder, with a strong recommendation for mercy on
account of his youth. With a black cap draped upon his wig, Mr Justice
Stable sentenced Richards to death as he stood unmoved in the dock.

A month later, an appeal, on the grounds that as the killing was an accident the trial judge should have allowed the jury to return a verdict of manslaughter, was made before the panel of judges at the Criminal Appeal Board in London. Dismissing it, Mr Justice Atkinson said that there was no evidence to support the appeal, as rightly the judge had pointed out that there was no evidence that Richards had pulled the trigger accidentally.

Owen Thomas Richards was returned to Walton prison, Liverpool, and Tuesday, 2nd December 1947 was set as the date for his execution.

As the date drew closer strenuous efforts were made to secure a reprieve and a petition was presented to the Home Secretary by Lady Megan Lloyd George MP, which contained many thousands of signatures.

With just 48 hours to spare it was announced that Richards would not hang, instead his sentence would be commuted to life imprisonment. He served just nine years for the cold blooded murder of his former lover.

11

TO SHOOT GAME AND WENCHES

THE MURDER OF DILYS SCOTT AT MARCHWIEL, MARCH 1950 AND OF CAROLINE EVANS AT COEDPOETH, OCTOBER 1945

Thirty year old Dilys Myfanwy Scott lived with her husband Harry at Cock Bank, a large farmhouse standing in its own grounds on the Overton road at Marchwiel, Denbighshire. Since their marriage in September 1946, Dilys and Harry had taken three rooms on the first floor, the rest of the house being occupied by Harry's widowed mother and three brothers.

On Thursday evening, 2nd March 1950, after having tea, Harry Scott went out into the field adjacent to the farm, where he got into conversation with his close neighbour, Mr Green. While talking, they heard the sound of an engine cut out and saw a single headlight from a motorcycle which coasted to a stop on the Overton road, close to the drive leading up to the house.

The two men continued talking for some time, until the sound of an explosion from the farmhouse set both of them running in that direction. As they approached the drive, the motorcycle fired into life and sped away in the direction of Wrexham.

Reaching the house they were joined by Harry's brother Kenneth who had been sitting in a back room, and entering through the front door, which stood open, they saw Dilys lying on the living room floor beside the sofa. She had been shot in the back and was dead.

The police were summoned and first to the scene was Inspector Charles Morris who travelled up from Ruabon. Inspector Morris found that there was no sign of a forced entry and no signs of violence other than the shots fired at Mrs Scott. Close to the body were three cartridge wads, one having a mark on it.

Dr Glyn Evans arrived later that night and examined the body. In his opinion, the doctor stated, the murder weapon was probably a twelve

Dilys Scott.

bore shotgun. Later that night Dr Walter Grace, the Home Office pathologist, carried out a post-mortem and found that death had been due to shock and haemorrhage caused by shotgun wounds to the back, which had also damaged the heart.

Inspector Morris returned to police headquarters and discussed the murder with Detective Sergeant Robert Woolf and Detective Constable Selwyn Jones. Jones was a local man and knew the Scott family well. He had made it his business to get to know any 'characters' in the area, and mention of a motorcycle being seen near the house immediately brought to mind the name of John Rusdell, a young soldier.

Cock Bank – an arrow indicates where Rusdell shot Mrs Scott.

Rusdell was certainly a 'character'. A trainee bandsman in the Parachute Regiment based at Aldershot, he was well educated, collected stamps, painted and drew with skill, and was an accomplished cello player. He had also a number of misdemeanours to his name, which had brought him into contact with the local police on several occasions. A quick check on his current whereabouts told officers that Rusdell had been back home on leave celebrating his eighteenth birthday on 24th February.

Orphaned at the age of three, home at Wrexham was with his adoptive parents Mr and Mrs Odgers, his aunt and uncle, whose house was at Burnham Gardens, Queen's Park. At 2.15 the next morning Detectives Jones and Woolf called at the house and spoke to John Rusdell in the presence of William Odgers. Rusdell was questioned about his movements between 7 pm and 8.30 pm on the previous evening and he told the officers he had spent the evening at the Odeon cinema where he had watched the film *A run for your money*. Asked if he could prove this, Rusdell said that he had spoken to the mother of an old schoolfriend, a lady he had known for many years, as they waited to go in.

Rusdell told the police that he had used his motorcycle to travel to the cinema, but added that when he returned to it at the end of the film, the engine was warm and he was sure someone had used it without his permission. William Odgers was able to confirm that John had returned home at 8.20 pm.

Detective Constable Jones asked Rusdell if he had passed through Marchwiel on the way home from the cinema. 'No!' he replied. Asked if he was certain he had not been in Marchwiel, Rusdell changed his story and said that he had ridden through the village on the way home and had seen a man dressed in black carrying what might have been a shotgun under his coat!

It was when John was asked if he owned a shotgun that William Odgers knew he was not telling the police the truth. The young soldier said he did not, but he did keep a Webley air rifle. Odgers knew this to be untrue for it was only a week or so ago when he had helped him saw down the barrels on the gun after Rusdell had told him it made it easier to shoot rabbits.

Mrs Odgers came downstairs and told one of the officers that she had sewn a special poacher's pocket on the inside of Rusdell's coat, and that last night he had asked her to remove it and take special care to remove all traces of the stitching. Mr Odgers gave police permission to search the house and within minutes a sawn down shotgun was discovered in a scullery sideboard. It had been recently fired and Rusdell was told he was being taken into custody pending further enquiries.

At Wrexham police station Rusdell made a statement in which he admitted he was trying to shield the real culprit, another local youth named Lionel Wynne Wilbraham. He said that during the previous afternoon the two travelled to Overton Bridge close to Cock Bank, where they had driven around sizing up the farm.

They had returned again that evening and had stopped outside the house. Wilbraham walked off saying he was going to get a drink of water. Rusdell asked him why he was taking the 'rod' (gun) with him, and was told that he might see a rabbit. He then walked up the drive towards the Scotts' farmhouse.

After waiting a few minutes, Rusdell claimed he heard a shot. He walked towards the house and saw the body of the woman on the floor as Wilbraham pushed past him and fled. He ended the statement by saying that he had failed to notify the police as it might be 'putting a rope around his (Wilbraham's) neck', instead opting to cover for his friend.

Questioned by the police later that morning, Wilbraham admitted knowing John Rusdell and that he had been with him on the afternoon of 2nd March. 'Rusdell told me he had a job planned for that night,' he told police, believing that his friend planned to carry out a robbery. They had parted at 3.50 pm and he had not seen Rusdell since.

Wilbraham told police he had spent the evening at choir practice at Coedpoeth. Mr Edgar Roberts, the choir master, confirmed that Wilbraham had been present between 6.35 pm and 8.30 pm, and there was no way he could have slipped out during that time.

At 3.15 pm that afternoon, John Rusdell was charged with the murder of Mrs Scott and remanded in custody. Asked if he had anything to say prior to being remanded, Rusdell replied: 'Yes sir, I would like to know where the other fellow is.'

Detectives searching Rusdell's bedroom found several books on crime, including one which Rusdell later said was his favourite, entitled *Down Murder Lane*. They also found a notebook in which he had written of his plans to commit the perfect murder. In his own handwriting were such phrases as '. . . go five miles to the end of the journey, then kill as you go back'. On the next page was a diagram of a house with two windows marked and the name 'Overton Road', along with the words 'You, you, walk kill.'

Rusdell admitted that the writing was his but claimed he had merely written down what Wilbraham had dictated. Rusdell said that his friend was a bit slow and had trouble writing.

The case against Rusdell was strengthened when his parents each made statements. Both claimed they were terrorised by their adopted son whenever he was home on leave.

William Odgers told police that Rusdell, who sometimes adopted an American accent and used phrases and expressions found in many popular gangster films, had told him while sawing down the gun that it would make it easier to kill with. He did not elaborate but it could have meant to kill people. Rusdell had also forced Mrs Odgers to sew the poacher's pocket on the inside of his raincoat in which he could conceal his gun, the same shotgun which he told his father would be ideal for 'shooting game and wenches'.

The police were now satisfied that there was a strong enough case and John Rusdell was committed for trial at the next Ruthin Assizes.

The prosecution counsel at the two day trial in May went over the evidence against Rusdell. They emphasised the writing in the note-book, dismissing the accused's claims that they were Wilbraham's words he had dictated, and claiming that these jottings proved it was Rusdell who had planned and committed the murder of Mrs Scott.

Mr Vincent Lloyd Jones KC, for the Crown, said Rusdell's visit to the cinema on the night of the murder was a carefully thought out alibi. He had deliberately made himself known to a witness who knew him well to put him at the cinema at 7 pm. He had then slipped out unseen and committed the crime, before returning home at the usual time. His manner on arrival aroused the suspicion of his parents, for he refused to eat any food, merely drinking cups of tea, into which he poured some rum as he was shaking.

Mr Lloyd Jones also mentioned a shallow grave which Rusdell had dug in his back garden, the purpose of which they could only surmise, but from what Rusdell had written in his notebook it appeared to have been prepared to bury the victim of his 'perfect murder'.

The defence counsel responded by trying to put all the blame on Wilbraham. Mr Glyn-Jones KC told the court that Wilbraham could easily have sneaked out of choir practice and committed the crime, and if as the prosecution had claimed it was a motiveless murder then there was no reason why Wilbraham could not have carried it out as well as Rusdell. They also made several veiled remarks about Rusdell's sanity.

After the judge had summed up the evidence, the jury considered its verdict and found Rusdell guilty. Mr Justice Austin-Jones, the trial judge, addressed the prisoner:

'John Lionel Raymond Rusdell, have you anything to say before sentence of death is passed upon you?'

Gripping the rail of the dock with both hands, Rusdell looked up at the judge and nodded.

'There is another murder you may be interested in. I killed Mrs Evans down Coedpoeth four years ago. I was only 14 then. Regarding the motive for this murder, it was sex.'

Suddenly, without warning, Rusdell hurled himself at a woman sitting close to the dock and then, overcome with hysteria, he had to be dragged to the cells below, his screams echoing around the courtroom. Ten minutes later, pale but now composed, John Rusdell was returned to the dock and sentenced to be hanged.

Initially the police made no comment on Rusdell's 'confession' from the dock, but it resulted in the re-examination of an unsolved, seemingly motiveless crime committed five years before.

Most Saturday nights attractive 38 year old Caroline Evans, a teacher at Wern infants' school, left her husband at their home in Coedpoeth and made the short trip on foot to stay with her widowed mother, who ran the City Arms pub at Minera a mile or so away. While her husband retired to bed at around 10 pm, Caroline would pack her overnight bag and set out in the darkness. On this occasion, Saturday, 6th October 1945, she never reached her destination.

Next morning her body was discovered lying in a thicket beside the path she had trodden many times before. The pathologist who examined the body told police she had been strangled and sexually assaulted; her clothing was torn and she was badly bruised, and in his opinion she had put up a fierce struggle before succumbing to her injuries.

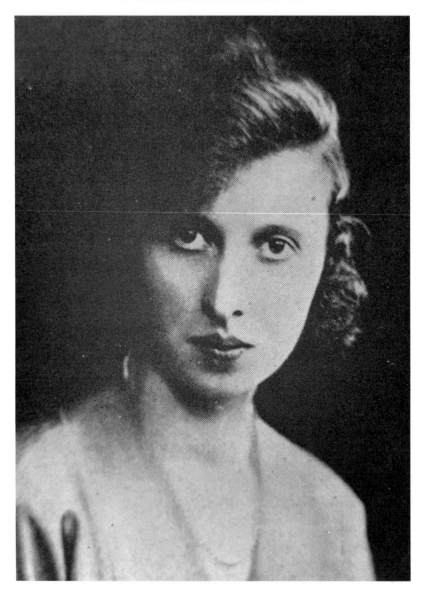

Caroline Evans.

As in every murder case, her husband, Edward David Evans, was asked to account for his own movements on that night so as to be eliminated from enquiries. He told the officer in charge, Chief Inspector Arthur Philpott of the Denbighshire Constabulary, that he was in bed when his wife had set out for her mother's. Explaining why she chose to arrive at such an unusual hour, Evans said that Caroline preferred to arrive after closing time because she did not think it right for a school teacher to be seen in a public house. He told the officer that he often offered to walk with her but she would not hear of it. The distraught factory clerk, ten years her senior, was quickly able to satisfy the police of his innocence.

It seemed to officers that there were two possible ways the teacher could have met her death. The first theory was that she had been stalked as she made the journey, with her murderer having planned the attack with precision. The second was that she had simply strayed into the path of someone with homicidal tendencies and had paid with her life.

The discovery of the body had been made at a remote spot known locally as Dark Hollow and a resident who lived close by told police that he had heard a piercing scream at shortly after 10 pm that Saturday night. He shone his torch in the direction of the noise but could see nobody.

Another witness, a miner from Minera, told police that he was crossing Dark Hollow at 11.30 pm when he saw the figure of a man in the bushes. He too carried a torch and shining it at the figure he could make out an RAF uniform with either one or two stripes on the sleeve. The miner said the airman was kneeling on the ground and seemed to dive forward to avoid being clearly seen. Thinking he had disturbed a courting couple, the miner apologised and walked on quickly.

This was a major breakthrough in the investigation as the airman had been seen very close to where Mrs Evans' body was found. Officers rounded up all RAF personnel in the area but each was able to be eliminated from their investigations as were those who had been present at the Saturday night dance at Coedpoeth drill hall, some 200 yards from where the path led to Dark Hollow.

The investigation progressed slowly. Police officers called at over a thousand homes in the area and despite taking statements from nearly everyone in the community, the identity of the killer remained a mystery. The net widened beyond Wrexham and then even further afield, but detectives still could not get the break needed to bring the killer to justice.

The mother of the victim, Mrs Harriet Williams, put up a large reward for information leading to an arrest, and although several people were taken into custody on suspicion and one man was arrested on the direct testimony of another, all were later released without charge. One of the major problems was the demobilisation of troops in the area. Almost daily, hundreds of servicemen were transferred from the region and the ending of hostilities also meant that there had been a relaxation in those soldiers having pass-outs from camp.

Gradually the hunt had to be scaled down. A murder case is never left unsolved and police were ready to step up the investigation if and when further evidence came to light. Rusdell's outburst from the dock brought Chief Inspector Higgins of Scotland Yard back to Coedpoeth to carry out further enquiries.

Meanwhile a month after the trial Rusdell's appeal was heard by the Lord Chief Justice (Lord Goddard), Mr Justice Humphries and Mr Justice Finnemore. The appeal was based on Rusdell's mental state, which was not fully referred to at the trial. Dismissing the appeal with his customary brusqueness, Lord Goddard stated it was unnecessary for them to go into the details of the case, and there was nothing for him to say except to dismiss the appeal.

Rusdell was returned to Shrewsbury prison to await his execution which was planned for 27th June 1950. Three days before he was due to hang, John Rusdell was reprieved, possibly because of his age, and his sentence commuted to one of life imprisonment. It was not long into his sentence when Rusdell was again examined by a panel of three Home Office appointed doctors with a view to his sanity and this time the panel certified him insane and he was removed to Broadmoor.

The City Arms, Minera.

Detectives searching 'Dark Hollow'.

Rusdell took up painting again while serving his sentence and on one New Year's Eve several years later, he smuggled some paint back to his room. The paint contained a large quantity of arsenic, and when guards later peeped into his cell John Rusdell was dead.

Did John Rusdell murder Mrs Evans at Coedpoeth? After the dramatic outburst in court, detectives re-examined the evidence over a period of many weeks. They reinterviewed many people and took further statements before finally issuing an announcement that John Rusdell did not murder Caroline Evans.

The mysterious murderer at Dark Hollow has never been brought to justice, and although technically an unsolved murder file is never closed, with nearly half a century having passed it is not unlikely that the killer of Caroline Evans, like the killer of Dilys Scott, has already gone to meet his maker.

12

LOVE AT FIRST SIGHT

THE MURDER OF EILEEN HARRIS AT FLINT,
DECEMBER 1951

Herbert Roy Harris met his wife to be, Eileen Humphries, shortly after his de-mob from the army. Although born in Coventry, Roy, as he was known to his friends and family, had lived in Flint since he was seven, and when called up he opted to join a Welsh regiment. During his stint in the army he served in both the REME and Welsh Guards Parachute Regiment.

Meeting Eileen was love at first sight. In his words, he 'fell in love the time I first set eyes on her, and had no interest in any other girl'. The courtship was swift and in 1948 Roy and Eileen married.

Finding a home was not easy in austere post-war North Wales, and as a result they were forced to live at a number of addresses in the first years of their marriage. They initially lodged with her parents on Queen's Avenue, Flint, while Roy finished an apprenticeship at a Chester engineering works, before moving on to Birmingham where they stayed with Eileen's sister. Perhaps as a result of being unable to settle into their own home, the Harrises frequently quarrelled, although each time they soon made up their differences.

They had not been long in Birmingham when Eileen announced that she was pregnant and, wishing the child to be born in her home town, they returned to Flint. Finding a family home was still a problem and soon after the birth of their first child, Susan, they separated for a time. During the next three years the couple had two more children, but their relationship was fraught with separations and quarrels, although as before each fight was followed by a swift reconciliation and promises that it would never happen again.

Late in 1950 they took two rooms at a house in the town while awaiting a council house they had applied for after the birth of their third child. Again they separated and each moved back in with their parents.

The separation seemed only to fuel the fires of reconciliation, and they would meet up perhaps three or four nights a week. Roy also began to save every spare penny in readiness for when they would receive their council house, and he spent all his free time making furniture for the house.

On Friday, 7th December 1951, Roy and Eileen met up during the day when he accompanied her to the dentist. They later did some shopping, picking up some items Roy needed to complete a bookcase he was building and which he intended to finish on the following afternoon. They separated later that day with a promise to meet up on the following evening for a visit to the cinema.

During the Saturday afternoon, Roy toiled hard to complete the bookcase and finished it just in time to have a quick bath before he went to meet Eileen. A little after 5.15 pm, he presented himself on her mother's doorstep only to find that his wife had gone to the cinema without him.

He hurried across to the cinema but as the film had started he was unable to gain entry. Roy decided he would confront his wife when the film ended, but in the meantime he would visit his grandparents who lived nearby. He bought a packet of cigarettes and called upon the old couple. They thought he seemed in good spirits when he bade them farewell and headed for The Ship where he drank a glass of stout before leaving to meet up with Eileen.

Roy was waiting in the cold as the cinema crowd spilled out. She smiled when she saw him and this seemed to stifle his anger. They walked away from the cinema, heading in the direction of Huntley bridge, and as they talked Eileen linked arms with her husband and put her head on his shoulder.

That same still, chilly December night Mrs Winifred Owen left her home at Huntley Lodge, Flint, to make the short journey to her daughter's house. It was shortly after 9.30 pm. Mrs Owen and her married daughter, Mrs Audrey Grogan, lived on either side of Huntley bridge, a narrow dirt road that spanned the main Chester to Holyhead railway line.

Stepping out into the bracing air, Mrs Owen approached the bridge, barely lit by the solitary gas lamp, and spotted at once the shape of a figure lying close to the wall. Situated less than a hundred yards from the busy Chester road, the area adjacent to the bridge was almost deserted, the only house on the river side being Huntley Lodge, the rest of the land taken up with fields.

Mrs Owen's first thought was that the figure was that of her daughter. 'Audrey! Audrey!' she cried out, hurrying onward. At first glance, her fears seemed to have been realised. The figure was clearly that of a woman, and the build, hair colour and coat were similar to those of her daughter.

Thinking she may have fainted, Mrs Owen lifted the woman's head and recoiled in horror when she found herself looking down upon the badly battered and bleeding body of a woman she recognised as Eileen Harris, whom she knew quite well. She ran screaming towards her home and summoned the police.

Officers were at the scene within minutes. First to arrive were Inspector Idwal Roberts and Police Constable Davies and a search of the immediate surroundings turned up a large bloodied stone. Police Surgeon Dr M. J. Quinlan was called and, examining the body, pronounced life extinct. Further officers arrived and under a powerful arc light, the body of the woman was removed to the local mortuary.

Detective Inspector Louis Allen from the Home Office forensic laboratory at Preston arrived with several of his officers and they removed a number of large bloodstained stones from the scene.

With the identity of the victim already established, police concentrated their enquiries on tracing the whereabouts of her husband. It was learned that he had returned home at 8.15 pm that Saturday night, changed his clothes and told his parents he was going out to meet Eileen. It was clear though, from what police had learned of the series of events earlier that evening, that at that time Eileen Harris was already lying dead on the deserted dirt track.

A search of Harris's room found that he had taken his savings – over £60 – with him, and officers wasted no time in alerting their colleagues in Chester and Liverpool, while a description of Harris was sent to every force in England and Wales.

The search for Roy Harris did not last long. He had boarded a bus to Chester from where he had booked a return ticket to London Euston. In the West End he booked himself into the Regent Palace Hotel signing the hotel register in his correct name. A routine police call to London hotels later that day soon had officers from the Metropolitan Police knocking on his hotel room door and he was placed under arrest.

Detectives from Flintshire caught the next train to London and on Monday morning Roy Harris began the journey north. He was taken immediately to Flint town hall where he was formally charged by the magistrate's clerk with the wilful murder of his wife on 8th December at Flint. Asked if he had anything to say, Harris replied: 'I have nothing to say except that it was not intentional, that's all.'

Two remands later, Herbert Roy Harris found himself before Mr Justice Oliver at Flintshire Assizes, Mold, on 4th February 1952. He was defended by Mr Glyn-Jones KC, assisted by Mr W.L. Mars Jones, whilst Mr Vincent Lloyd Jones KC led for the Crown, assisted by Mr Bertram Richards. Smartly dressed in a dark suit and light brown overcoat, he pleaded 'not guilty' in answer to the charges and a packed courtroom heard the Crown put forward its case.

Herbert Harris and his wife.

Mr Lloyd Jones referred to a statement Harris had made shortly after his arrest in which he described what had happened on that fateful night: 'I was angry because she had gone to the cinema without me. Eileen said to me: "If you don't like the way I do things you can clear off and keep away from me." She struck me on the chest. I struck her with my hand and she rushed at me screaming. I lost my temper and picked up a big stone and threw it at her and she fell to the ground. Seeing blood on my clothes I stumbled down the avenue home.'

This statement, the Crown claimed, was proof that Harris had committed wilful murder. He had battered his wife to death with a large stone after losing his temper following a quarrel.

The prosecution also stated that several large bloodstained stones had been examined and evidence suggested that it was the largest of these, weighing over 50 pounds, that Harris had picked up and dropped on his wife's head. This tied in with the evidence given by Doctor Walter Grace, the Home Office pathologist, who had earlier described how the dead woman's skull had been shattered in over ten places.

The crux of the prosecution's case rested on the fact that when Harris struck the fatal blow he intended to kill his wife. Mr Lloyd Jones concluded by saying that the evidence they had heard showed that this was clearly the case, and that in fleeing to London he had hoped to escape the consequences.

Defence counsel Mr Glyn-Jones asked the jury to consider the state of the prisoner's mind when he struck that blow. Was the provocation so great as to reduce the crime to manslaughter? He demonstrated that Harris was of previous good character, with an exemplary army record. He finished by saying that Harris's vagueness on answering some of the prosecution's questions was because he was genuinely traumatised by events on the night of the murder, which had been the doings of a man in a frenzy. In closing, Mr Glyn-Jones said that although Harris had fled to London he had done so because he was scared and once there had made no effort to conceal his whereabouts.

After listening to the judge's summing up, the jury needed just 48 minutes to find Harris guilty of murder, although they added a strong recommendation for mercy. A black cap was draped over Mr Justice Oliver's head as he passed sentence of death upon the prisoner. As the priest concluded the dreaded sentence with 'Amen', Harris's mother, sitting with her husband just behind the dock, collapsed and had to be carried out of the courtroom.

The condemned man was removed to Strangeways prison, Manchester, to await the hangman while petitions were started in Flint and the surrounding districts. There was no appeal, instead his counsel pinned all their hopes on a reprieve. This failed as did a last ditch plea to the Home Secretary for clemency. The execution was scheduled for Tuesday, 26th February 1952. On the Monday evening, as hangmen Albert Pierrepoint and Robert Stewart silently rigged the gallows, Harris received a last visit from his parents and brother.

On the stroke of nine o'clock next morning, the hangmen entered the cell. Stewart noted in his diary that Harris showed no sign of fear as they entered and he smiled as the straps were fastened around his arms. Seconds later Herbert Roy Harris had paid for his crime.

13

THE GUN CANNOT LIE

THE MURDER OF ADA ROYCE AT HOLT,
DECEMBER 1951

The still calm of a cold winter Saturday night, 29th December 1951, was shattered by the sound of two gunshots fired in quick succession. Amongst the few folk making their way home along Castle Street, the main thoroughfare through the sleepy border village of Holt, were brothers William and Frank Bithell who were returning home after a drink in their local pub. Up ahead walked their sister Ada Royce and Frank's wife Ellen.

The brothers stopped in their tracks at the sound of gunfire, then hurrying through the semi darkness they found themselves looking down upon the body of their sister lying bleeding in the gutter. Close beside her was the wounded figure of a man well known to the brothers, Harry Huxley.

Other couples making their way home initially thought the sound was that of a firework, but by the commotion further ahead it was soon apparent that something serious was afoot.

Ada Royce, a 32 year old mother of three, lived on the recently constructed Dee Park estate at Holt with her husband Harry, who was at home at the time of the shooting. Her brother Frank and his wife lived next door.

It was clear to the distraught brothers that Ada was already dead when they reached her, while Huxley was bleeding heavily from a self inflicted gunshot wound to the left side of his chest. A metal buckle on his braces had diverted the bulk of the charge away from his heart, preventing him from taking his own life, and a police officer, Sergeant Moss, accompanied the wounded man as he was removed to Wrexham War Memorial hospital.

Surgeons operated on the injured man on the following morning and removed numerous pellets from his chest. Later that day, as he lay recuperating in the hospital bed, Harry Huxley was charged with the wilful murder of Mrs Ada Royce on the previous night.

Ada Royce.

The White Lion, Holt.

Inspector C.L. Morris of the Denbighshire police force, who was assigned the case, unearthed a story of unfaithfulness, deceit and unrequited love which had culminated in the brutal shooting late that Saturday night.

In 1940 Ada had married Charles Henry 'Harry' Royce and within a year she had given birth to a son, George, and two years later a daughter, June, was born. Unable to afford a home of their own, they took a room at her mother's house.

In 1945 Huxley was discharged from the army and on the night of his de-mob, while at Farndon, he saw Ada Royce whom he had known for some years. Huxley proceeded to get very drunk and was later helped home by Ada. From then on he became a frequent visitor to her house. In September 1946, the Royces separated for a short time as a result of Huxley's repeated visits to the house. It appeared that her mother was aware of Huxley's visits and on more than one occasion had covered for her daughter.

Royce confronted Huxley, a single man living with his mother, who worked as a labourer on the same industrial estate where Royce worked as a machinist. He warned him not to call at the house while his wife was alone.

'Are you accusing me of being after your wife?' Huxley asked.

Newspaper cutting depicting the scene of the shooting in Castle Street.

Royce replied that he was not accusing him of anything without proof, but in his opinion he was only going to the house to be with his wife.

'Fancy you thinking I was a fellow like that. If my mam got to know about this, it would kill her!'

Relations between Royce and his wife improved when they moved into their own home but her affair continued and when she gave birth to a third child in 1947, a son she named Tony, she told Huxley that he was the father. As a result he regularly gave her money towards the child's upkeep.

Whether Harry Royce knew that Huxley was reportedly the father of his youngest child was never made clear, but relations between himself and his wife remained good right up until the day of the tragedy.

On Christmas Day 1951 Huxley met Ada Royce in the Gredington Arms, Holt. Relations between the two had cooled in recent months and it appeared that lately she had gone to great lengths to avoid contact with Huxley.

Earlier that afternoon he had called on a farmer friend and asked to borrow a shotgun and cartridges. Asked why he wanted a gun, Huxley said it was to shoot pheasants. Handing the gun over, the farmer warned Huxley that the right hammer was faulty and for him to take care.

Later that night Ada Royce was sitting in the Gredington Arms with her sister-in-law, Ellen Bithell. Also in the bar was Huxley and after insisting that they took a drink with him, the girls quickly downed a shandy before leaving him and taking a seat in the lounge. Huxley was then seen to carry two glasses of port over to the women and place them down on the table. They had not asked for the drinks and they stayed on the table untouched.

A little while later as they were about to leave, the women saw Huxley in the other bar. He was waving what appeared to be a shotgun over his head. None of the regulars seemed to be concerned by this behaviour; when sober Huxley was known to be meek and inoffensive

Castle Street as it looks today.

and although he pointed the gun at several people no one took much offence, realising he was very drunk. Later people had to step over him as he lay drunk on the steps outside the pub.

At 9.20 pm on 29th December, Huxley was in the White Lion at Holt. Also in the bar were Ada and Ellen Bithell. At one point Huxley asked Ellen to go outside. What transpired outside is unclear but from something Huxley later told a friend after returning to his drink, the fact that Ellen Bithell apologised for not accepting his drink on Christmas Day probably saved her life. Huxley followed up this statement by opening his coat and showing his friend the shotgun. He was slightly drunk by this time.

At 10 pm, the women left the White Lion and walked home down Castle Street. They stopped off at the chip shop and Huxley who had tagged along persuaded Ada to buy him a bag of chips. Throughout the short walk to the shop, Huxley was bemoaning the fact that they had not accepted his Christmas drink.

Finally she snapped. Huxley had just told Ada that he had had a gun with him on Christmas Day and if he had been sober he would have shot her for refusing to drink with him. Ada had clearly had enough of his pestering and said that she was going to report him to the police.

Ellen walked on ahead as Huxley grabbed Ada by the arm. They spoke for a minute by which time Ada's brothers had arrived on Castle Street and were following behind. Suddenly there were two shots and Ada lay dead in the road.

Harry Huxley recovered from his injuries to stand trial at Ruthin Assizes in May 1952. He was defended by Miss Rose Heilbron QC, assisted by Mr Bertram Richards, while Mr Edmund Davies QC prosecuted, assisted by Mr W.L. Mars Jones. Mr Justice Croom-Johnston presided.

The case for the prosecution was that Huxley had intentionally killed Ada Royce, carrying out a two part plan he had had in his mind for some days. The second stage was that he should kill himself.

A letter was read out in court which had been found in Huxley's possession when taken into hospital. It was addressed to Harry Royce and signed 'W.P'. It read:

'Dear Harry,
Just a line to let you know that my wife was down Holt at Christmas and she was told about your wife. She is not playing the game with you, and that she meets the same man, and another thing, that one of the kids belongs to him, so keep a look out and don't be soft. I will tell you more when I see you in town - from your old pal.'

The prosecution alleged that this letter had been written by Huxley with the intention of trying to break up the marriage of Royce and his wife thereby leaving her free to be with him. The motive for the killing

Shrewsbury prison.

they then alleged was the unwillingness of Mrs Royce to leave her husband and be with the prisoner.

In his defence, Miss Heilbron claimed that the gun had gone off by accident and that Huxley had not intended to commit murder. Realising, in horror, what he had done, he had turned the gun on himself in an unsuccessful suicide attempt.

Miss Heilbron pointed to a statement in which the farmer who had lent Huxley the gun had warned of the faulty firing mechanism. Detective Inspector Louis Allen of the forensic science laboratory at Preston backed up this point, pointing out that marks on the raincoat indicated that the gun had been fired at point blank range. This the defence claimed supported the suggestion that the gun had gone off accidentally on contact.

Miss Heilbron asked Detective Inspector Allen: 'If the gun was in a man's hand and he knocked it against the woman's clothing, that might cause it to go off?'

'It might do.'

'It is a gun very liable to go off accidentally?'

'That is my opinion with regards to the hammer.'

'Very likely to go off accidentally?'

'Yes.'

Concluding her defence, Miss Heilbron asked the jury to put aside their feelings on the morals of the case, adding this was not a 'court of morals' and in a last dramatic attempt to plead her case, she picked up the murder weapon and addressed the jury: 'Witnesses can tell untruths, but this gun cannot lie!'

The jury filed out, returning two hours later to find Huxley guilty of murder. Addressing the prisoner before passing sentence, Mr Justice Croom-Johnston told him: 'After a most careful and anxious trial, the jury have obviously accepted the plain evidence which is against you.'

Harry Huxley was hanged at Shrewsbury prison on 8th July 1952.

14

THE INNOCENCE OF MRS ROBERTS

THE SUSPICIOUS DEATH OF JOHN ROBERTS AT TALSARNAU, MARCH 1952

It had seemed a harmless enough prank. 'Smart widow wishes to meet widower aged about 48. Children no objection. Write Box C. 621', read the advertisement in a Holyhead newspaper one spring morning in 1950. But whatever its original intention, it was almost certainly the catalyst that was to lead, two years later, to a middle-aged woman standing trial for murder.

It would be perhaps an understatement to say that Alicia Hughes had led a traumatic life. Born in Dublin in 1900, she was two years old when her father deserted her mother and emigrated to Australia. After finding work as a clerk, her mother uprooted the family and moved across the Irish Sea, settling in Holyhead.

The Great War was almost over when Alicia fell in love with Emrys Williams, a young soldier home on leave. After a brief courtship they became engaged and fixed their wedding for 27th August 1918, but ten days before she was due to walk down the aisle, she received notice that her fiance had been killed in action. Emrys Williams was given a full military funeral at Holyhead and his bride-to-be's wedding dress became his burial shroud.

In 1922 she met John Hughes, a demobbed soldier. Hughes had suffered badly in the war and as the result of a heavy gas attack he was never in good health, his chest in particular was to give him trouble for the rest of his life.

Alicia married John Hughes at Holyhead in 1923, and a year later she gave birth to a son Owen Richard, whom she affectionately called 'Dicky'. Despite her husband's ill health, they were happy enough together, although Alicia's dreams of having a large family were cruelly shattered when after a major operation she was told she would be unable to have any more children. They decided to increase the family by adoption; in 1939 they adopted a baby girl, Diana, and in late 1948 they adopted baby Marlene.

The happiness of the new arrival was soon overshadowed when John Hughes was confined to bed with a serious illness. His condition worsened and on Monday, 6th June 1949, he passed away. Death was recorded as due to a chronic chest complaint.

Alicia tempered her grief by devoting herself to bringing up the two young children, a task which she was able to combine with her newly found job as a caretaker in a local church hostel.

The first Alicia Hughes knew about the newspaper hoax was when the postman handed over a large bunch of letters – 62 in total – each addressed to 'The Advertiser'. The bemused widow, who never learned the identity of the prankster, read each in turn before throwing them all onto the fire. All except one.

Written by a 44 year old widower, Jack Roberts of Talsarnau, Merionethshire, something in its contents struck a chord with the maternal, homely widow, and rereading it later, she wrote out a reply.

John Gwylym Roberts, or 'Big Jack' as he was known locally, lived with his five children in a four-roomed cottage at Talsarnau, a slate roofed village situated at the foot of Mount Snowdon. The cottage was tied to the adjacent school, and in return for maintaining and taking care of the school. In his letter he told her about his young children, that he had been a widower for five years and that during that time the family had been looked after by his eldest daughter, now 20, who was due to leave home to take up a job in Birmingham.

Alicia dispatched her letter and received a reply by return. They arranged a meeting at a mutually convenient place and found they had much in common. More letters followed and shortly after Christmas he asked her to be his wife.

Although a certain amount of affection had built up between the couple, it was clear it was to be a marriage of convenience for both parties. Not only was he gaining a wife, but also a mother for his children; while on her part, the school house at Talsarnau would provide a new home for Alicia and her children, as she was due to lose her current home when the church hostel was closed down. Losing her home and a job she enjoyed had been another painful blow which, like the many others over the years, Alicia had learned to take in her stride.

Shortly after Jack Roberts' proposal, Alicia travelled to Talsarnau to consider her decision. One look at the pitiful scene was enough to persuade her to accept the offer, and on 3rd March 1951, they married at Blaenau Ffestiniog.

She soon realised that she had gotten the rough side of the bargain. Her husband and eldest stepson rose at dawn and set out for work as railway gangers, while before tending to the school boiler room the new

Mrs Roberts would have to make breakfast for the children, pack them off to school and tend to the mountain of dishes and dirty washing.

Life became one round of chores and when Jack's eldest daughter Doreen wanted to return home to resume her role as lady of the house, Alicia was faced with hostility, both from Doreen and several of her relatives. Doreen Roberts had been unhappy with her job in Birmingham and wrote to her father asking to come home. However, the routine she had left behind had changed drastically and fearing the inevitable conflict between his new wife and eldest daughter, Jack advised Doreen against returning for the time being. Doreen, it seemed, blamed her stepmother.

In January 1952, Alicia Roberts called to see the family doctor. In tears she admitted she was very unhappy with the marriage and it was making her ill.

Matters then came to a head when Doreen, having ignored her father's request not to return home, wanted to bring a large Welsh dresser into the already crowded cottage. It was a legacy left by a relative, but Alicia was adamant that it was not coming into the house. They quarrelled and she told her husband, 'If that comes, I go!' Instead of backing up his wife, as she asked him to, Jack Roberts, torn between wife and daughter, threatened to commit suicide. It would later prove to be a significant threat.

On 4th March, Jack Roberts was taken ill. His wife nursed him and the doctor was called. Dr Hogg, the same family physician Alicia had opened her heart to only a few weeks before, knew from old that Roberts was a hypochondriac, but the symptoms he was displaying, severe vomiting and abdominal pains, seemed genuine enough.

The next morning Roberts was fed a breakfast of porridge and a short time later he was again violently sick. The doctor agreed to call on the following morning. After another call later that afternoon he prepared a tonic for Roberts, but by the time he called at the school house on the following morning, Jack Roberts was dead.

Perhaps remembering the conversation with Mrs Roberts, and aware that the symptoms displayed by the dead man were similar to those of poisoning, Dr Hogg refused to sign a death certificate and reported his suspicions to the local coroner.

As a result of this, pathologist Dr Edward Gerald Evans was asked to perform a post-mortem. This he did at Bangor infirmary and sent a number of organs to the forensic science laboratory at Preston where a report was prepared that stated the cause of death to be acute arsenical poisoning.

Unaware of the investigations going on in Bangor and Preston, Mrs Roberts began arrangements for her husband's funeral and on the evening of 11th March, in the company of her son Dicky, she went to see Dr Hogg. Police called at the surgery and questioned Mrs Roberts about the traces of poison found in the body of her husband, and during the questioning she asked to visit the lavatory. When she failed to return after a time, police entered and found her unconscious on the floor: she had cut her throat and both wrists with a razor. She was quickly ferried to the Bangor infirmary where she was found to have sustained only minor injuries.

Having suspected foul play, police had already launched an investigation which found that Mrs Roberts had purchased two tins of arsenic based weedkiller from a chemist in Porthmadog shortly before her husband's death. It was found that she had signed for the poison using a different name, and on 3rd April 1952 Alicia Roberts was charged with the murder of her second husband by administering arsenic poison. She was also charged with unlawfully attempting to commit suicide by cutting her throat. She was held in Strangeways prison, Manchester while the case against her was put together.

A few weeks later a preliminary remand hearing was held at Ffestiniog court to see if there was enough evidence to go to a higher court. Evidence was heard regarding the purchase of the weedkiller. The children of the dead man also took the stand and claimed that their stepmother had taken to giving her husband porridge shortly before his death, and each time he ate this he became violently sick.

Based on testimony of Mrs Roberts that confirmed she had purchased arsenic prior to her husband's death, the short hearing found that there was indeed a strong case against her and she was remanded to stand trial at the next assizes.

On Monday, 8th July 1952, Alicia Roberts stood before Mr Justice Ormerod at Swansea. The case against her looked very strong and the Crown was led by one of the leading prosecutors, the Attorney General Sir Lionel Heald. He was to be assisted by Mr Glyn-Jones QC, while Mr Edmund Davies QC and Mr F. Elwyn Jones appeared for the defence. The jury of nine men and three women listened as the Crown opened proceedings.

With the tins of weedkiller clearly visible on the table before him, the Attorney General outlined the case. John Roberts died on 6th March 1952. Immediately before his death he was suffering from symptoms consistent with those of acute arsenical poisoning – violent stomach pains, vomiting, diarrhoea and a severe thirst. His doctor was not satisfied as to the cause of death and analysis of internal organs found he had died from arsenical poisoning and no other cause.

It all looked very black for the accused as she sat forlornly in the dock. Fortunately she had able counsel and they went to work straight away, tearing into the case. One slip the prosecution had made was to subpoena Dicky Hughes to give evidence against his mother. He

82

followed his stepbrothers and sister into the dock, but instead of backing up their evidence that his mother had recently introduced porridge for breakfast, he claimed this to be untrue and that it had been a common breakfast over the recent months. He also contradicted them on several other points and it was a definite victory for the defence. He was one of 20 witnesses called by the Crown.

Rebutting the prosecution counsel's assertion that there was no evidence to support the accused's claim that she had used weedkiller in the gardens of the school house, Mr Edmund Davies called two key witnesses. Firstly, James Clark, the city analyst of Liverpool, told the court that he had taken samples of soil from the gardens of the old school house at Talsarnau and analysis revealed they contained 70 parts per million of arsenic – approximately half a grain per pound of soil. Evidence indeed that someone had treated the garden.

This was further supported by horticulturalist Harry Lodwig Jones, who also examined the garden soil and stated that there was evidence to suggest that arsenic had been applied to the path at the school – exactly where Mrs Roberts claimed she had purchased the poison for.

There was a further scare for the defence when under questioning Mrs Roberts admitted she had tried to hide the evidence of the tins of weedkiller after her husband's death. Asked why she had done so, Mrs Roberts said: 'It struck me that something might be thought different to what was right.' It seemed a very weak excuse, and the defence claimed it was weak because it was the truth, inferring that someone with a more sinister motive would have thought of a better explanation.

The defence suggested that Mr Roberts could have taken the poison deliberately in an act of suicide, the dosage found in the body suggesting that a large, and presumably fatal, dose had been ingested just prior to his death. The Crown could find no witnesses who had seen Mrs Roberts administer the poison, nor was there any suggestion that the children had poisoned their father. The only reasonable assumption, therefore, was that Jack Roberts had taken the poison for reasons known only to himself.

One of the most sensational Welsh trials in modern times ended on the third day. After both counsel made closing speeches the judge summed up the evidence and invited the jury to consider a verdict. Almost four hours later they filed back into court and announced that they found Mrs Roberts not guilty of murder. Her son collapsed in a faint at the verdict, the strain of the trial finally taking its toll.

Mrs Roberts set foot outside the court a free woman but it was not to be the end of her ordeal. Not just yet.

Investigations into the death of her first husband had also revealed traces of arsenic in his decomposing body, which had been exhumed after her arrest. Was it just coincidence that two husbands had died

Mrs Roberts hugs her son after being cleared of murder.

from self-administered arsenic poison or was there something more sinister?

An inquest was scheduled at Holyhead for a fortnight after her acquittal, and wary of the suspicions against their client which at worst could lead to a second murder trial, her counsel engaged the services of the most eminent pathologist of the day, Dr Francis Camps, to work on their behalf.

Mrs Roberts' lawyers were briefed that the Crown had called Dr Roche Lynch to check samples of soil from the grave at Holyhead. Sixteen years earlier, Dr Roche Lynch had played a prominent part in sending another Irish born housewife, Charlotte Bryant, to the gallows for poisoning her husband with weedkiller. At first glance the two cases had many similarities.

Dr Roche Lynch's findings indicated 13 parts of arsenic per million in the soil around the coffin. There were also traces of arsenic in the muscles and bones of the decomposing body, and in the water that filled the coffin.

In his opinion, Dr Roche Lynch claimed, 'the remains contained an abnormal amount of arsenic which cannot be accounted for by contamination by external sources after death. Thus I am of the opinion that an administration of arsenic must have accelerated death in this case.'

This was a devastating claim and one that would, naturally enough in the circumstances, be sure to raise suspicions and might well be enough to send Mrs Roberts back to the dock. Her lawyers were also aware that she might not be so fortunate this time and could face the very real possibility of the hangman's rope. Especially since the Crown intended to call witnesses to say that prior to his death John Hughes had suffered stomach pains and diarrhoea.

Fortunately, Dr Camps was one of the best in the business and after reading through Dr Roche Lynch's statement he felt sure that he could rebut it.

Asked at the inquest if he agreed with Dr Roche Lynch's findings, Dr Camps said he disagreed. 'Because of the state of decomposition,' Camps said, 'it is impossible to ascertain the cause of death. Insoluble arsenic washed into the coffin from the soil could have adhered to some of the body such as the brain and muscles and still have been present at the time of analysis.'

Asked by the defence if there was any evidence to suggest that John Hughes had died of arsenical poisoning, Camps replied: 'I would not be prepared to support the theory on the evidence today. The cause of death was quite consistent with natural causes.'

As with the murder trial, Mrs Roberts gave her counsel some nervous moments. Following her son into the witness box, and after hearing him

Dr Camps.

say he had never seen weedkiller at the Holyhead home, Mrs Roberts admitted buying some weedkiller on 26th May 1949, two weeks before her first husband's death. This brought an audible gasp at the inquest. 'I have nothing to hide,' she went on. 'I signed the poison book and used it in the garden.'

Delivering their verdict, the coroner's jury sided with Mrs Roberts. Just. It seemed that Camps had done enough to cast doubt about the actual cause of death, and after deliberating for a little under an hour the jury returned an open verdict. In other words they suspected that a crime may have been committed, but they could not specify who was to blame.

Walking from the coroner's court a free woman, Alicia Roberts made a statement. 'It may seem that some suspicion could be levelled against me, but my heart and conscience are clear.'

Did a guilty murderess escape conviction? Had she been convicted of either murder Alicia Roberts would almost certainly have gone to the gallows. Yet despite what looked like overwhelming evidence the testimonies of two experts who found arsenic in the school gardens at Talsarnau had swayed the jury at Swansea, and the authoritative evidence of Dr Camps had done enough to spare Mrs Roberts a second murder trial.

One suspects that had she faced a second murder trial, with the evidence of the first trial still fresh in the minds of even the most unbiased jury, the odds of a second acquittal would have been very long indeed.

15
PRIME SUSPECT

THE MURDER OF ELIZABETH ANNE STEPHENSON AT HAWARDEN, OCTOBER 1957

It was 8.30 pm on Tuesday, 1st October 1957, and Police Constable Ben Davies was patrolling his beat in Queensferry, Flintshire, when he noticed the stationary car close to the police station. Opening the door, the driver gestured for the constable to climb in and Constable Davies saw that the man was shivering, covered in mud and had several scratches on his face, one of which was bleeding. The driver stared through the front windscreen for several moments then turned to the officer and spoke in a whisper. 'I am upset,' he said, before lapsing into silence and again staring ahead through the windscreen.

Something was clearly wrong and PC Davies asked the man to accompany him into the station where he asked what had upset him. The man said there was the body of a boy in a ditch down the road.

While the desk sergeant summoned assistance, the officer and the driver left the station and flagged down a passing taxi driven by James Washington who, after dropping off a fare, was on the way to his home in Ellesmere Port. Constable Davies asked the taxi driver to take them to a spot on the Queensferry to Chester road at Sandycroft.

Reaching the scene the men searched the road using the light from the car's headlamps but it was not until PC Cox of the motor patrol arrived with several powerful torches that they found the body of a girl, not a boy as first thought, lying on her back in the ditch. Together, the two officers managed to pull her out of the slimy, stagnant water.

Within a short time Inspector Hugh Williams and Sergeant William Wynn Lloyd of Connah's Quay arrived at the roadside, accompanied by Dr Michael Gavin, and after confirming that the girl was dead the body was transferred to Connah's Quay mortuary.

The man who had discovered the body had given his name as Gerald James Cooke, a 32 year old crane driver of Shotton, employed at the De Havilland aircraft factory at Broughton. He also told them he was married and had two young sons.

Elizabeth Stephenson.

Gerald Cooke shows police where he discovered the body in the ditch.

He made a statement describing how at 7.45 pm, while driving to work on the night shift, he saw a movement in the vicinity of the ditch on the right-hand grass verge and went to investigate. The shape had looked white and bulky and stopping the car he walked back and heard splashing and gurgling coming from the ditch. He realised there was a person in the ditch when he saw a hand come up, and he then tried unsuccessfully to get them out of the water.

He returned to his car in shock at what had happened, especially as he had received a scratch to his face, and sat down in a daze. Twenty minutes later, having got himself together, he had driven to the police station.

The identity of the dead girl was discovered: she was 16 year old Elizabeth Anne Stephenson who lived with her family on the 'Little Roodee' RAF station at Hawarden. Anne, as she preferred to be known, was originally from Lisburn in Northern Ireland and had only been in Flintshire for two months. Her father, Flight Lieutenant George Stephenson DFC, had recently been installed as the Flight Commander at West Kirby RAF station and the family had moved into the area from Lincolnshire.

Anne worked as a sales assistant at Chester Arts and Crafts studio and had returned home from work by bus earlier that evening. After tea, Anne and her 14 year old brother Tony went out for a walk, but as Tony had promised to do his homework they parted at 7. 20 pm and he left his sister to walk on alone. Tony last saw his sister alive as she walked along Sandycroft Road towards Queensferry. She was wearing a white duffle coat and tight black trousers.

When Anne failed to return home later that night the family drove around the area looking for her, presumably passing the police as they started up their investigations, before reporting the matter at their local police station. In the early hours, George Stephenson had the unpleasant task of identifying his daughter's body at Connah's Quay mortuary.

From the outset, police were suspicious of Gerald Cooke. His story did not quite ring true. Almost from the first moment he became the prime suspect, and a close watch was kept on him.

Witnesses were sought who had travelled down Sandycroft Road on the previous night and police soon had some very clear leads. A number came forward to say they had seen the young girl walking down the road. Each put the time as between 7.40 pm and 7.50 pm, and police appealed for passengers on the 7. 27 pm bus from Flint to Chester to come forward, as it had passed by the scene at around the time Cooke claimed to have been struggling in the ditch.

As more and more witnesses came forward, holes began to appear in Cooke's initial statement. More than one person mentioned seeing a man park his car and walk back towards the girl as she walked beside the road. A motorcyclist gave police a good description of the man seen walking towards the woman, wearing a fawn mackintosh coat and with greased down hair. Cooke had been wearing a similar coloured mac when he reported the incident.

Police questioned Cooke several times during the next few days, and he even posed for a press photograph pointing to the spot where he had tried to save the girl.

Inspector Williams was assisted in his enquiries by two officers from Liverpool CID, Detective Chief Superintendent James Morris and Detective Superintendent Harold Welsh, and Inspector Cecil Williams of the Flintshire CID. Together the officers arranged a reconstruction at the ditch using a life-like model. Police Constable Davies was selected to try to remove the model from the ditch in the manner Cooke had described, and it was found unlikely, though not impossible, that Cooke would have struggled in the way he suggested.

It was also suspicious that the girl should be unable to haul herself out of the water-filled ditch if she had slipped in accidentally. She was a strong girl and a good swimmer, who would have had little problem climbing out of the water if she was not being prevented from doing so by someone.

As the investigation progressed it seemed more and more likely that that someone was Gerald Cooke, and one week after the tragedy police called on him at work and charged him with murder.

By the time the case came to court in the following February the Stephenson family had returned to their native Ulster and they travelled back to watch their daughter's killer as he stood in the dock at Flintshire Assizes, Mold.

Mr Roderick Bowen QC, prosecuting, said that at 9 pm on Tuesday 1st October the body of Elizabeth Anne Stephenson had been recovered from a ditch alongside the Sandycroft Road, between Queensferry and Chester. It was found that she had been dead for a short time and following a post-mortem it was revealed that the cause of death was asphyxia due to inhalation of mud.

The prosecution suggested that Cooke had driven past the young girl as she walked home alone and he had pulled up and walked back towards her, perhaps with the intention of committing a sexual offence. Cooke had waited until the road was clear before he dragged her off and into the ditch, but as he tried to force himself upon her a bus approached, and in order to hide from view he forced the girl into the muddy water. During the struggle he received a scratch to the face and when he left the scene Anne Stephenson was dead. Cooke had then spent 20 minutes in his car thinking up a plausible story which he offered to the police.

Defence counsel, Mr Mars Jones QC, stuck to the original story that the accused had seen the girl struggling and had tried to rescue her. Failing to do so, he became distraught and had panicked. That was the only reason he had delayed in calling the police.

Medical evidence was given by Dr Gerald Evans who told the court that when he examined Anne's body her face was coated with mud, like a mud pack, and after carrying out tests it was found that mud only stuck to the face if the body was pushed into the ditch backwards. This, the prosecution alleged, was further proof that the victim could not have got into the ditch accidentally.

The five day trial ended on Friday, 7th February when after retiring for less than an hour the jury found the prisoner guilty as charged. Mr Justice Glyn-Jones then sentenced Cooke to life imprisonment.

16

THE DEATH OF A WAR CRY GIRL

THE MANSLAUGHTER OF MAIR JONES AT RHOSLLANERCHRUGOG, JUNE 1958

Twenty year old Mair Jones was a well known figure in and around the Rhos area. More often than not dressed in her Salvation Army uniform and bonnet, she was a frequent sight in any number of clubs and public houses where she would sell copies of the Salvation Army newspaper *War Cry*, and in one or two of the pubs she was even known as the 'War Cry Girl'.

Mair's parents had split up at an early age and she had been brought up by her grandparents. This family disruption had affected her schooling and she had done badly in the classroom, being thought by her parents and teachers somewhat backward. Since the death of her grandmother she lived alone with her grandfather at Good View, a detached house on Pant Lane, Rhos.

On Friday night, 6th June 1958, she visited her mother and stepfather who lived nearby. The purpose of this visit was to say farewell for the immediate future, as Mair had taken up a summer job at Barmouth and was due to leave on the following morning. They talked for a while and parted at 10.45 pm, with Mair opting to walk the short distance home. She never arrived.

Next morning at 7.15 am, Phil Philips, a 73 year old retired miner of Stryt-issa, Penycae, was out walking his dog Toss. Approaching the gateway to Pant brickworks he saw, resting in a hollow and lying on some barbed wire, what he thought was a tailor's dummy. On closer inspection he found that he had stumbled across the body of a young girl. He was joined by a passing newspaper boy who draped his cape over the body and then rushed to call assistance.

The first officer to reach the scene was Sergeant Neville Jones of the Denbighshire police force, based at Rhos. One look at the body was

Chief Constable Rees (centre) beside the covered body of Mair Jones.

enough for the officer to recognise the victim. He had known Mair Jones and her family for many years and was now faced with the unpleasant and unenviable task of breaking the terrible news to her relatives.

It was also clear that Mair had been the victim of a brutal sexual assault. This much was evident from the state of her dress: she was naked from the waist down and her remaining clothing, a dark blue dress and grey check coat, was roughly dishevelled. Mair also had blood caked around her nose and on her forehead.

Later that afternoon Detective Superintendent Richard Lewis took charge of the investigation and immediately called in Dr Edward Gerald Evans, the Home Office pathologist. Dr Evans left his home at Bangor and hurried to the scene and later that afternoon carried out a post-mortem.

Mair was five feet two inches tall and slightly chubby. Her tongue was protruding from her mouth and her fingernails, toenails and earlobes were all a deep shade of blue. This, the vastly experienced doctor saw, was consistent with death due to asphyxiation. There were no bruises to her thighs, but there were a number of blows to her face and on her lower arms.

Dr Evans also found that Mair had been sexually active and that

Mair Jones.

Terence Jones.

death could have been caused by someone applying pressure on her chest or on her mouth and nose, perhaps during sex. Death this way could have been so quick as to have been measured in seconds rather than minutes.

Working on the assumption that Mair may have walked to the brickworks with her killer, police set about interviewing anyone who had been in the Pant Hill and Penycae area the previous evening. Scores of statements were taken and as a result police questioned 20 year old Terence George Jones, a haulage hand at Bersham colliery, who lived with his parents at Penycae.

Jones was spoken to as he left the cinema on Broad Street on Saturday night, and was asked to accompany Inspector Berwyn Jones and Sergeant Davies to Rhos police station. He later accompanied the officers to Llangollen station where he was questioned about events of the previous night.

'Do you know a girl named Mair Jones?' Superintendent Lewis asked him.

'Yes, I went to school with her,' he replied.

Asked if he had seen her on the previous night, Jones replied: 'No.'

He was then asked to account for his movements and told police that he had met up with two friends and gone drinking in the King's Head, Rhos. They drank a large amount of beer in a number of pubs before setting off for home eventually taking the road for Penycae. The statement ended: 'I have been asked if I know Mair Jones. Yes I know her, but I did not see her last night.'

It was as he signed the statement that the Superintendent noticed a number of scratches on his arms. They appeared to be fresh but Jones claimed that he had received them at work during the previous week. The Superintendent then spoke slowly and clearly to Jones, telling him that he wanted the doctor to examine the scratches while he went to check on the statement.

Jones looked at the officer for a while and then put his head in his hands and broke down.

'I didn't mean to do her any harm, sir,' he said, before making a fresh statement, this time admitting meeting Mair as he walked home. 'The parts I have told you already are true but I missed this part out.

'I followed Mair up the cinder track. After I caught her I put my arm around her and we walked for a couple of hundred yards together. My mate, Frank, was walking close behind me. We stopped on the corner just before her home.

'Then Frank came to us and we both pulled her down like. We were laughing and joking. She started screaming. Frank put his hand to her mouth. I held her hand with one of mine. When she fell down her clothes came up. Frank was on top of her sitting on her. She started squealing like I said. When Frank put his hand over her mouth he stopped her squealing.

'She started kicking and trying to squeal, and Frank kept trying to stop her squeal. His hand was over her mouth.'

Jones said that he then came to his senses and realised what he was doing: 'I got up and ran back towards the way I had come. I stopped to see if Frank was coming. I could see that he was not coming so I walked back quietly to meet him.'

As Jones approached his friend Frank jumped up and said: 'Come on, let's get out of here.' Jones continued: 'We run for about 200 yards then walked the rest of the way. I went with Frank to his sister-in-law's house. They were in bed when we got there. There weren't any lights on.'

Jones then told how after they had returned to his house and after a cup of tea they parted and he went to bed. Next morning his mother woke him up and told him that a girl had been killed at Pant brickworks. 'It's a girl, but they can't recognise her face,' she told him.

Jones carried on by saying that he had called to see Frank who had also heard about the girl's death. 'I asked him if he had done anything else other than put his hand over her mouth, and he said no, all I did was hold her hand and put my hand over her mouth to stop her screaming.'

Jones said that they went for a ride on Frank's motorbike that Saturday afternoon and more than once he (Jones) suggested that they faced up to what had happened, but Frank insisted that they denied any involvement. 'That's why I didn't tell you about it. When I told you about the scratches I didn't want to be untruthful. I think I got them from the barbed wire when she fell down.'

Referring to the victim, Jones said that he had never been out with her before but said that she was noted as a 'rum character'.

Following this statement, officers interviewed Francis Joseph Regan 'Frank' Schleising, a 25 year old salesman. He kept up the pretence of not knowing the dead girl and made a statement giving an account of his movements on the previous night.

Supt Lewis looked him in the eye and said that it was his duty to search for the truth and he wanted to give him every opportunity to tell everything he knew. 'I believe you to have been at Stryt-issa last night,' the officer said, to which Schleising replied, 'Have you seen Terry?'

When told he had, Schleising asked if he could be told what his friend had said and was told 'No'. He then made a statement which mirrored in many ways that of Jones.

On 9th June, both men were charged at Ruabon police station with the murder of Mair Jones. Asked if they had anything to say, Jones replied, 'We didn't go there with that intention.' 'That's right,'

Schleising added, 'We didn't intend to commit it.'

The case was heard before Mr Justice Havers at the Denbighshire Assizes held at the historic Ruthin County Hall on Monday, 13th October 1958. Mr Vincent Lloyd Jones QC led for the prosecution whilst both accused had two defence counsel; Jones being represented by Mr Mars Jones QC and Mr Ronald Waterhouse, while Schleising was defended by Mr Elwyn Jones QC MP and Mr Robin David.

The Crown pointed to the statements both the accused had made when arrested. In the dock, Schleising told the court that when he and Jones had left the girl they did not think she had come to any harm. 'I did not think she was unconscious or dead. I thought she would be able to go home.'

Schleising said that he and Jones had followed Mair as she made her way home. He said he thought that his friend was on a 'good thing' and he would merely wait at the end of the lane for them. He quickened his pace to keep up with them and they then fell down onto the ground. It was when the girl started screaming that he made efforts to silence her.

Dr Evans gave evidence that it was these efforts that had resulted in the death of Mair Jones. Speaking for over two hours, the pathologist reiterated what he told Supt Lewis after carrying out the post-mortem, that death would have been quick if enough pressure was applied to prevent her breathing.

Summing up the case for the prosecution, Mr Lloyd Jones QC invited the jury to agree that Jones was every bit as involved in the ill treatment of the unfortunate Mair Jones as Schleising. It was Jones who took advantage and was in a position to see exactly what was happening.

Speaking on Jones's behalf, Mr Mars Jones urged the jury that there were three verdicts open to them: firstly, a verdict of guilty of murder; secondly, a verdict of manslaughter, and thirdly, a verdict of not guilty. He submitted that there was little dispute about the general events of that fateful night and that fuelled by drink the two men decided to have sexual intercourse with the girl, if necessary against her will.

'No evidence suggested that Jones did anything which caused the death of the girl,' he said. 'Jones engaged up to a point in a joint enterprise and he was certainly a party to the rape or attempted rape while the girl was being held down by Schleising.'

Ending his address, Mr Mars Jones said evidence had suggested that the girl died after Jones had run away and if the jury decided on this they could find him not guilty. 'But if you find against him on that issue then the verdict must be murder or manslaughter; I invite you to say that it was manslaughter.'

Schleising's counsel concentrated on showing that their prisoner was of previous good character, unused to drinking heavily, and it was the drink that had caused him to carry out the assault. 'I am not here to

Francis Schleising.

excuse Francis Schleising for what he did that night,' he said. 'The combination of a sudden sexual lust with intoxication of an unaccustomed amount of liquor was responsible for these deeds which they will regret to the end of their days.'

It was as Mr Elwyn Jones made this closing remark that Jones collapsed in the dock and had to be carried from the court. Finishing his plea, he told the jury that if they believed his prisoner guilty then the verdict should be one of manslaughter.

After debating their verdict for one hour, the all male jury filed back into the court and announced that they found the pair not guilty of murder but guilty of manslaughter.

A hushed court heard Mr Justice Havers address the prisoners before passing sentence. 'This is one of the gravest cases of manslaughter. You followed this poor girl who was on her way home with no one to help her. You treated her with the utmost brutality and you left her not knowing whether she was alive or dead. It is true that it was Schleising's hand that actually caused the death. You, Jones, are equally guilty. You knew what he was doing and took advantage of it. Both of you are a disgrace to a civilised society.'

He then sentenced both men to eight years' imprisonment. A large crowd flocked around the courtyard exit as a prison van took both prisoners to Shrewsbury gaol to start their sentences, no doubt ruing that one moment when they let their animal instincts get the better of them.

17

THE MUMMY IN THE CUPBOARD

THE SUSPICIOUS DEATH OF MRS FRANCES KNIGHT AT RHYL

For nearly 20 years Sarah Jane Harvey, a 65 year old widow, had made a weekly visit to the local post office to collect pension money for both herself and her friend and former tenant, Mrs Frances Knight. Many years earlier Mrs Knight had lodged with Mrs Harvey at her small terraced house on West Kinmel Street, Rhyl, but with her health failing she had moved into an old folks' home at Llandudno to see out her twilight years in supervised comfort.

That was the story Mrs Harvey had told the staff at the post office and whenever asked about her friend, she would say, 'Oh, she's not been too good', or 'She's a little better', always promising to pass on their kind remarks when she next wrote or visited.

Sarah had been widowed following her husband Alfred's death in 1938, and from that time the house had played host to several lodgers, the first of whom was Mrs Frances Alice Knight, the wife of a Rhyl dentist. Some 20 years older than Sarah, Frances was estranged from her husband and when he uprooted and moved to Brighton in 1936, she had taken a room with Mrs Harvey.

One spring afternoon in 1960 Leslie Harvey decided to treat his mother's house to a springclean and fresh coat of paint. After an illness, Sarah was confined in the local hospital for a series of tests while doctors monitored her progress.

On Thursday, 5th May 1960, Leslie Harvey finished work a little earlier than usual and along with his wife left their home at Abergele and travelled to Rhyl, calling at his mother's house armed with some cleaning materials. As his wife busied herself in the kitchen, Leslie walked around estimating how much wallpaper and paint would be needed to complete the job.

The house on West Kinmel Street had been Leslie's home until he married in 1958 and as he still kept a key the redecoration was planned as a surprise for when his mother left hospital.

Climbing the narrow staircase, Leslie's attention was drawn to the large pine cupboard at the top of the stairs. He thought back to the many times over the years he had wondered what was inside this cupboard, which had always been locked. He recalled asking about its contents once, some years earlier, and had been told by his mother that it contained clothing and other items belonging to some wartime lodgers which she was looking after until they could arrange for collection.

With screwdriver in hand, Leslie slipped the blade against the lock and prised open the door. What he hoped to find one can only guess. Perhaps some battered luggage and out of date clothes, or maybe some nice, long-forgotten pieces of silver?

As the door creaked open a musty smell filled his nostrils, and shining his small flashlight torch he recoiled at the sight that greeted him. From something huddled in a ball, covered in cobwebs and old flypapers, Leslie could clearly make out the shape of a human foot. He called for his wife to take a look and they quickly went to fetch her father who lived close by. He returned with the couple and after verifying that it was indeed a human body, they summoned the police.

Officers hurried to the scene in the company of the local police doctor. One look by him was enough to know that it was a job for a specialised pathologist and later that evening Dr Gerald Evans arrived at the house accompanied by Dr Alan Clift of the forensic science laboratory at Preston.

The two doctors found that the mummified body was so hard that it had stuck fast to the wooden cupboard floor, and as a result a shovel was needed to free it. This was a nauseating job for the pathologists as every time the body moved it disturbed clouds of dust.

An inch by inch examination was made of the body, which was clearly that of a woman. Generations of flies had long ago feasted on the tongue, eyelashes, stomach and other internal organs, while moths had destroyed the hair and clothing. The skin was peppered with maggot holes but there was a distinctive groove on the left side of the neck. The mummy was removed to Preston where it was cleaned up and experts set about putting a name to the body.

This had been the first question police had asked Leslie Harvey. Did he know the identity of the mummy in the cupboard? Thinking long and hard, he recalled a elderly widow who had lodged there during the war. He said her name was Mrs Knight and that she had been in her mid-sixties and was partly crippled.

One can only surmise what went through Mrs Harvey's mind as detectives visited her bedside on the following day. At the first visit she feigned total surprise. Officers left her while they followed up further

Sarah Jane Harvey.

enquiries and the next time they returned to the hospital they mentioned the name of Mrs Knight.

Sarah Harvey was now faced with a dilemma. Police had discovered that she had been collecting Mrs Knight's pension money and sending it on for the last decade or so, so she could hardly claim not to know the current whereabouts of Mrs Knight. She gave police an address at Llandudno but when officers went to check it out they merely exposed a lie.

Questioned again, Mrs Harvey offered to tell the truth. She told detectives that Mrs Knight had lodged with her during the war and that as she became old and frail, she found it hard to walk. One night Sarah found her lying on the bathroom floor in tears. 'I am in pain and would rather be dead,' she told her. Sarah said that she tried to lift her off the floor but was unable to do so, and after going downstairs to make a cup of tea she returned to find her lodger had died.

She went on to explain how she became scared because there was no one else in the house and in a panic she had dragged Mrs Knight's body across the landing and put her in the cupboard. Chief Inspector Williams, listening to this statement with other senior officers, could not help but think that if she was strong enough to drag Mrs Knight along the landing, then she should have been able to lift her off the bathroom floor.

What she had not taken into consideration was that the conditions inside the airing cupboard were almost perfect for preserving the body, the constant stream of hot air recreating the same effect as the desert climate had upon the Pharaohs' corpses inside the Egyptian pyramids.

The officers were also taken aback by the callousness of the old woman, as Mrs Harvey went on to describe how she had first hung fly-papers in the cupboard and then wedged an eiderdown against the body after locking it inside the pine cupboard. She had taken in numerous lodgers over the following years and had continued to draw pension money for both herself and Mrs Knight.

It was when forensic evidence found traces of a ligature around the mummy's neck that police began to suspect foul play. Cleaning up the body they found what appeared to be the remains of a knotted stocking tied around the neck, and working on the assumption that the mummified corpse belonged to Mrs Knight and that she had been strangled, the investigation became a murder case.

The post-mortem turned up a number of pointers that led police to believe the mummy was indeed that of Frances Knight. Working to the latest formulae for estimating the height of the body in life, Dr Evans calculated her height to have been approximately five feet four inches. He also stated that her blood group had been group O and she had been aged between 40 and 60. Mrs Knight matched this finding on every point. Three days after the discovery of the body, Sarah Harvey was arrested and charged with murder.

When Mrs Harvey stood dwarfed between burly prison guards in the dock at Ruthin Assizes in the autumn of 1960, she was fortunate to have excellent counsel in Mr Andrew Rankine and Mr Somerset Jones. Prosecuting were the Solicitor General, Sir Jocelyn Simon QC MP, assisted by Mr Elwyn Jones QC MP and Mr Bertram Richards. Presiding over the trial was Mr Justice Davies.

Opening the case, the Solicitor General claimed that the accused, by her own showing, was a cool and accomplished liar, an elderly widow with nerves of steel, but it was greed that led to her standing trial for murder. The Crown contested that Sarah Harvey had strangled Frances Knight for the sake of a small weekly amount of pension money.

The Crown also pointed out that if the death of Mrs Knight had been anything other than murder, then Mrs Harvey could simply have reported the matter to the police and the whole matter would have been cleared up at once. Was she afraid that the matter might have been investigated further?

After all, enquiries turned up the startling fact that seven previous occupants of 35 West Kinmel Street, Rhyl, had died during a period of 15 years leading up to the Second World War. All the victims had been aged around 60 plus years old so their deaths had perhaps not aroused any undue suspicion, but as two occupants had already passed away in 1940, when the pathologists had concluded that Mrs Knight may have met her death, a third sudden death could have been enough to warrant further investigation.

The defence challenged the cause of death, calling in the brilliant pathologist Dr Francis Camps. He offered the theory that the ligature was nothing more sinister than an old stocking which had been tied around the neck as an old wives' tale to ward off a cold. The 'cure' was popular in certain parts of the country and it was believed that the dirtier the sock or stocking, the quicker the cure.

It was clear from the forensic evidence that the victim had been in ill health suffering not only from the cold but from disseminated sclerosis. Although there was enough evidence to suggest that the disease was not yet in its fatal stages, it would have only been a matter of time before this was the case.

The defence, who had failed in an effort to cast doubt as to the identity of the mummy, then offered the theory that the extent of Mrs Harvey's crime was merely to conceal her lodger's death in order to benefit by claiming the money. Whatever thoughts she had had when she first set this plan into motion were unclear, but it became a situation that once she had gone ahead with, she was unable to alter. The longer she covered up the death, the more money she received. In the period

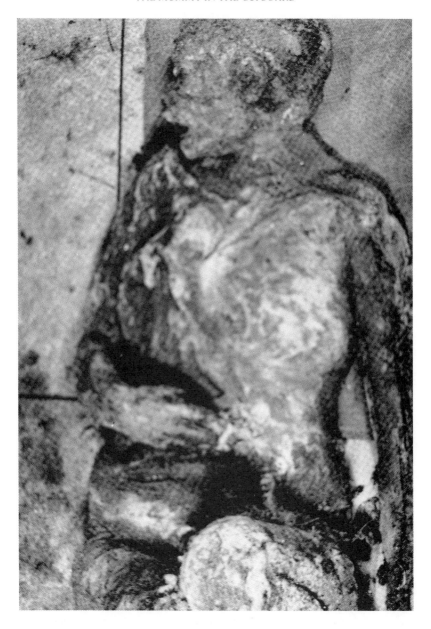

The mummy after being cleaned up at the lab.

between Mrs Knight's death until the discovery of the body Mrs Harvey had claimed over £2,000.

When the trial ended on the fifth day of proceedings it was something of an anti-climax. As the prosecution evidence ended and the court took a recess, counsel had a brief conference. Both sides agreed that the prosecution's case was weak. Even Dr Evans who had carried out the investigation on behalf of the Crown said he was unable to state for certain that the ligature around the neck had caused the death, nor was he even sure if the stocking had been put on before or after death, although using a cold cure on a corpse would surely be a pointless exercise. It came down to the fact that if the Crown could not prove that the stocking had caused death then there was no case.

The defence admitted that the accused had brought about the trouble she found herself now in, and the judge concurred. Instead they offered a plea of obtaining money by deception and on this count Mrs Harvey, who was not in good health throughout the trial, was sentenced to 15 months' imprisonment.

18
AN ACT OF MADNESS

THE MURDER OF MARGARET HUGHES AT MENAI BRIDGE, JUNE 1961

Margaret Gregory Hughes had spent the evening with her parents at the family home at Penycraig, Llangefni. The attractive 21 year old had for the last nine months been employed as housemaid to Doctor Henry Fisher and his wife at Llys Merion, Menai Bridge, a post that came with her own room at the doctor's surgery.

On Friday, 30th June 1961, Margaret left Llangefni and returned to Menai Bridge, alighting from the bus shortly before 11 pm. As she crossed the square in the direction of the surgery on Water Street, she was accosted by a foreign sailor.

'Are you not afraid to go home alone in the dark at this time of night?' he asked her in broken English. Margaret did not answer and walked on quickly.

Next morning, at a little before 9 am, Dr Fisher's wife knocked on Margaret's bedroom door. There was no reply. She knocked again, this time entering as she called out. Sunlight streamed through the thin curtains and there lying on the bed was the naked and ravaged body of Margaret Hughes. Mrs Fisher's screams alerted her husband and rushing into the room the horrified doctor saw at a glance that their maid was dead.

The police were called and later that morning Dr Gerald Evans, the Home Office pathologist, carried out a post-mortem at Bangor infirmary. He found that the victim had been sexually assaulted, raped, and had suffered various head and facial injuries. Death was due to asphyxia.

Lieutenant-Colonel W. Jones Williams, the Chief Constable of Gwynedd, immediately organised a full-scale investigation and asked for assistance from Liverpool CID.

Investigations at Menai Bridge revealed that a timber-carrying motor vessel, *Weima*, had sailed earlier that morning bound for Liverpool and detectives were sent to the port to question the crew.

Officers at the murder scene soon found a wealth of clues. It was clear that whoever had committed the brutal murder had gained entry to the house by climbing through a small window in the bathroom. Clearly visible in the bathroom were footprints, in both the bath and on the window sill, the sole pattern on the shoes was the 'bar type' similar to that on a basketball shoe.

Also on the window ledge were a clear set of fresh fingerprints and after eliminating prints legitimately expected to be there, this left one set of prints that must belong to the killer. The same rogue set of prints were also found on the bedroom door, inside the room, and on recently broken tiles on the outhouse roof.

On Sunday evening the crew of the *Weima* were interviewed and fingerprinted, and the tell tale prints were seen to match those of 29 year old merchant seaman Hendrikus Wilhelmus Rumping, a native of Amsterdam. Rumping was detained in police custody and in the early hours of Monday morning he was interviewed by Detective Inspector Humphrey Jones and Detective Sergeant Evans.

The officers told Rumping they were investigating the murder at Menai Bridge and asked him if he understood English. He said that he did and he was then taken from Liverpool to Menai Bridge for further enquiries.

At 10.45 pm, that Monday night, Inspector Jones formally charged Rumping with murder. Although the Dutchman had a fair grasp of English he was granted an interpreter and a Dutch-speaking Holyhead businessman was asked to do this task. Rumping's solicitor, Mr Emyr Parry of Caernarfon, said that Rumping would apply for legal aid as he had no means of his own. The prisoner was then removed to Walton gaol, Liverpool, to await trial.

Hendrikus Rumping stood trial for murder at Chester Assizes on Monday, 23rd October 1961. Mr Justice Hinchcliffe presided. Mr Alun Davies QC, prosecuting, said that Margaret Hughes was strangled between 11.30 pm and 3.30 am on 1st July.

Rumping, who pleaded not guilty, made a statement in which he admitted going ashore on the Friday evening. He said he spent the night drinking in the Liverpool Arms Hotel, leaving at closing time. He then met up with two crew mates and after purchasing a bottle of milk from an automatic machine in the square, they returned to the ship at 11.40 pm. 'I was a little drunk and did not go ashore again,' Rumping claimed.

The time that Rumping returned to the ship was crucial to the prosecution's case. A crew mate, Gerrit Van der Hoek, confirmed Rumping's estimation of the time they reached the ship but under examination by counsel he admitted that he could not be sure of the exact time, and it could have been as much as an hour later than he first stated.

Hendrikus Rumping's ship was moored in the Menai Straits.

Next to give evidence was Dr Gerald Evans, who confirmed that the time of the murder was as stated earlier. He had estimated this time after taking hourly temperature readings on the body on Saturday morning. Questioned by Mr Philip Wein QC, counsel for the defence, however, Dr Evans was forced to concede that the times were only approximate and that death could have occurred as late as 4.30 am.

Dr Evans also stated that despite the extensive number of blows to the face, along with bruising on the neck, he could not say for certain that Margaret had been raped, although as the judge at this moment pointed out it did not seem likely such extensive injuries could have been inflicted on a consenting person.

A witness then gave evidence in which he identified Rumping as the man he had seen follow Margaret down the street and overheard speak to her after she had alighted from her bus, and another witness also testified that he had seen a man matching Rumping's description standing in an alley close to the doctor's surgery on two previous occasions earlier in the week. Asked when arrested if he knew the victim, Rumping merely shook his head.

Evidence from Rumping's shipmates revealed that he had been seen washing his clothing on Saturday afternoon and that he no longer seemed to own the pair of basketball shoes he had worn throughout the

Dr Gerald Evans who carried out the post-mortem on Margaret Hughes.

rest of the week. Rumping later admitted throwing a pair of these boots into the Menai Straits because 'they were broken'.

One of the most damning pieces of evidence against the accused was supplied by his own hand in the form of a letter he had written to his wife and which he had given to a crew mate to be posted when the ship returned to Rotterdam. When Rumping was arrested the seaman passed the note to the skipper of the *Weima*, Captain Johan Belstra, and he in turn handed it to the police who had the contents translated.

Before the note was read out in court the defence asked the judge to rule the letter as inadmissible evidence as there was a principle of common law that communications between man and wife, which were not intended to be disclosed to others, were protected from disclosure in court. After considering the request for over an hour, Mr Justice Hinchcliffe ruled that the letter was admissible as evidence and its contents were read to the court:

'The Irish Sea, July 1, 1961
My dearest wife.

I have done something in an act of madness you will never be able to forgive me; what it is you will learn later on.

When you receive this you will perhaps never see me again. If people ask you just tell them about my fits of rage and that I do things that I never remember doing afterwards.

I wish you the very best in your life; give me a little thought once in a while. I love you.

Hendrikus.'

This letter, the prosecution stated, was as good as a confession to murder. Further evidence against the accused was supplied by forensics. A number of human hairs found on and beside the victim matched those of Rumping, as did a number of fibres found at the murder scene. Defence challenged this last point but their expert was later forced to agree that the fibre could have come from the accused.

The final evidence was supplied by fingerprint expert Chief Inspector George Weeks of Liverpool, who pointed out that Rumping's prints, one of over a thousand sets taken during the short investigation, were a perfect match to those found at the scene.

The defence made a valiant effort in the face of the overwhelming evidence but the five day trial ended with the jury finding Rumping guilty of non-capital murder. Mr Justice Hinchcliffe sentenced him to life imprisonment.

His appeal against conviction was heard in the following summer but the court concurred with the original finding and the appeal was dismissed.

19

MURDER IN THE HAPPY VALLEY

THE MURDER OF JUNE ROBERTS AT WREXHAM, AUGUST 1962

The tree-lined yard at the rear of the one-time school canteen, now a bakery, on Whitegate Road at Hightown, Wrexham, was a popular courting spot for couples to head for after a night out. So popular in fact that neighbours had long since learned to shut out the occasional screams and shouts that along with other verbal intrusions became something of a nuisance once the warm weather came around.

It was just after six o'clock on the morning of Bank Holiday Saturday, 4th August 1962, when a resident on Hampson Avenue entered his kitchen and put the kettle on. Looking out of his back window, which overlooked the bakery yard, he saw what he thought to be a drunk lying near two of the bakery vans. He called for his son to dress and come down, and together they crossed the yard and found the partially clothed body of a girl.

The two men hurried home to call the police but by the time officers had raced to the scene, the owner of the bakery had arrived to open the works. Unaware that the police were on their way, the owner's attention was taken by what appeared to be red paint splattered across the wall close to the front door. As some painters had been working at the bakery he did not pay too much attention to this, but when he entered the yard at the rear of the premises he discovered the body. He was about to call the police when a patrol car pulled up at the gates.

Even the experienced officers were shocked by the brutal and pitiful sight that confronted them. The Chief Constable of Denbighshire, Mr A.M. Rees, took charge of the investigation and assigned a number of his officers on house to house enquiries while others combed the bakery yard for clues.

It was apparent that the victim, whose identity at this stage they were still to ascertain, had suffered terrible head injuries, inflicted in the

The scene of the crime.

alcove close to the front door. This was the spot where the bakery owner found what he thought were spots of paint. It appeared that she had been the subject of a sexual assault before her body was then dragged to the rear of the yard. A lady's black shoe was found near the alcove and a number of buttons from her blue woollen coat were also found scattered close by.

It was a matter of course that the Denbighshire police force called in Scotland Yard on murder enquiries and later that Saturday night Chief Superintendent William Tennant and Sergeant Ernest Cooke of the Murder Squad left London and travelled up to Wrexham. Reaching the town, they joined their Welsh colleagues in a conference where they were briefed with details of how the investigation was progressing. Chief Superintendent Tennant had only been with the Murder Squad for three weeks and this was to be his first major murder enquiry.

In the meantime, pathologist Dr Gerald Evans travelled from his home at Bangor to carry out a post-mortem on the victim, whose identity had now been established as 23 year old June Roberts of Connor Crescent, Hightown.

A diminutive, frail redhead, weighing a little over six stone, June was the eldest of five children and lived with her parents in the family home

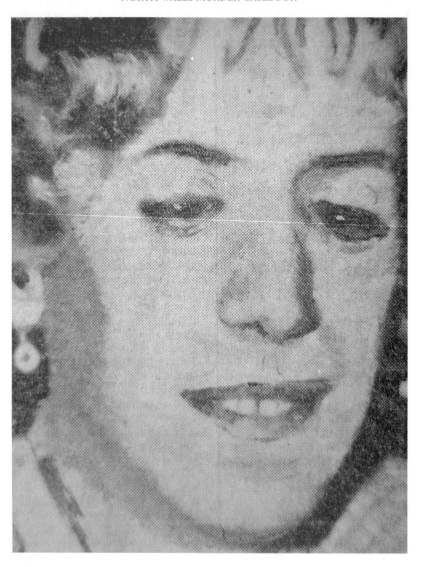

June Roberts.

Chief Superintendent Tennant and Sergeant Cooke shortly after arriving at Wrexham to investigate the murder.

less than 200 yards from where she was found murdered. Dr Evans stated that cause of death was from severe head injuries, adding that she had also been raped.

It was learned that her father, Charles Roberts, had seen June in the company of a young man as he made his way home from the pub on Friday night. He had spoken to the couple as they strolled together and although the youth had spoken to Charles and offered him a cigarette, the light on the street was not good and other than saying he wore a dark suit, Charles was unable to give police a description of the man. He had, after all, been drinking quite heavily himself that evening.

Charles had left his daughter and the youth as they approached the bakery, asking her, 'Isn't it time you were coming home?' June told him she was old enough to look after herself and after promising to lock the door but wait up for her, Charles left the couple and walked home.

When June failed to return home in the early hours both her parents put on their coats and walked the streets hoping to find her. The early morning visit by the police saw their worst fears realised.

Investigations revealed that June was fond of a drink and a sing-song

117

Terence Hughes.

and had been drinking with friends in a number of pubs in and around the Queen's Park area of Wrexham. She was a popular figure and had friends from both sexes and police spent many hours questioning the movements of the men, several of whom had spent some of the early evening drinking with June. Each was able to account for his movements.

Several people mentioned seeing the young man police believed may have been the man Charles Roberts saw with his daughter. Aged between 18 and 20, he had a short 'army style' haircut and wore a dark suit. One suggested a name and two officers worked on tracing the whereabouts of this man.

Officers at the scene searching for the victim's missing handbag discovered a piece of broken drainpipe which had a number of bloodstains upon it. It was dispatched to the forensic science laboratory at Preston to see if it could be the murder weapon. A report suggested that it was possible that this pipe had been used in the attack.

Fortunately for the frightened town, the killer of June Roberts was under arrest within the week. Acting on information supplied, 18 year old Terence John Hughes, a soldier in the 1st Battalion Royal Welch Fusiliers, was arrested late Monday afternoon. Hughes was stationed at Salisbury but was home on leave and staying with his parents who lived at Queen's Park, Wrexham.

Hughes had spent the Bank Holiday with unsuspecting friends at a caravan park near Prestatyn. Clearly sporting a number of abrasions, he had told his friends he had gotten into a scrap in a local pub and although they had all heard the news of the murder at the Hightown bakery before setting out on the short holiday, no one for a minute considered that Hughes might be behind it.

Hughes was arrested by Detective Sergeant Charles Matthews and two constables of the Wrexham CID in a Gwespyr public house. At almost the same time, Hughes' father was putting away some clean washing in his son's room when he discovered a bloodstained raincoat and trousers in a drawer. These were handed over to the police and the blood was found to be the same group as the dead girl, group A. Hughes' blood group was O.

A large crowd gathered on Regent Street on Wednesday morning as Hughes was bundled into Wrexham police station, where he was questioned by the Scotland Yard officers. He made a statement denying any involvement with the crime but, under further interrogation, he finally admitted the murder. 'It was me,' he said, 'I did it.' Later that afternoon he was formally charged with the murder of June Roberts and remanded in custody.

Hughes had given officers his version of events on the night. He described how they had walked through the grimly ironic 'Happy

Valley' area of Hightown, where they happened upon her father. After bidding him goodnight, they entered the bakery and began to kiss when in his words, 'I went sort of mad and started hitting her. I dragged her around the corner to where there were two vans and left her there.'

On the following Friday, June Roberts was laid to rest at Wrexham borough cemetery, following a service at St John's church, Hightown. Hundreds of people congregated to pay their respects including the officers who had two days previously taken her killer into custody.

The trial of Terence John Hughes at Denbigh Assizes, Ruthin, in October that year was notable only for the briefness of the whole proceedings. Lasting less than two minutes, and with just a hundred words spoken, Hughes, dressed in a smart blue suit, calmly pleaded guilty to the crime.

Hughes replied 'No, sir,' when asked if he had anything to say before sentence was passed. Mr Justice Howard then told him that there was but one sentence ordained by law for this offence: 'that you be imprisoned for life'. He was granted a brief visit by his elder brother and father before being escorted away to start his sentence.

Back in London, Chief Superintendent William Tennant was involved in another investigation when he heard that Hughes had been convicted. He would surely have been gratified that the team had achieved such a quick result on his first murder case.

20

DEATH ON ST DAVID'S DAY

THE MANSLAUGHTER OF KAREN POOLEY AT COLWYN BAY,
MARCH 1986

It was a civil servant exercising his dog who made the gruesome discovery. Strolling across deserted wasteland close to the main Liverpool to Holyhead railway line at Colwyn Bay, he spotted a bundle lying on the frozen ground and, gingerly approaching, found himself staring down upon the body of a young girl. It was a cold Sunday morning, 2nd March 1986.

The dead girl, dressed in a pink skirt and blue anorak, was naked from the waist down, with her legs bent double beneath her. It appeared that no effort had been made to conceal the body and the man wasted no time in raising the alarm.

Detective Chief Superintendent Gwyn Owen immediately took charge of the investigation. The victim was identified as 18 year old Karen Pooley, who shared a flat with her boyfriend at the Rothesay Hotel, West Promenade, Colwyn Bay. A happy-go-lucky girl, she had recently left her family home in Aigburth, Liverpool, to find work in the North Wales holiday resort.

Detectives discovered that Karen had intended to spend the night out with her boyfriend, but when he failed to return after spending the early evening drinking in a local pub, she went out alone. She spent the early part of Saturday night at the town's 'Flight Level Zero' discotheque at the Metropole Hotel, before rounding the night off at the Imperial Hotel. Both hotels had been packed with revellers celebrating St David's Day and Chief Superintendent Owen assigned over 60 detectives to interview anyone who might give them a lead as to why Karen met her death.

Later that afternoon, Home Office pathologist Dr Donald Wayte carried out a post-mortem and ascertained the cause of death as manual strangulation. Dr Wayte stated that pressure had been applied on the victim's throat for approximately three minutes, effectively ruling out any chance of it being anything other than a deliberate, premeditated act.

Dr Wayte told detectives that the girl had also been subjected to a brutal sexual assault and he noted the peculiar and unnatural way in which Karen's body lay when discovered. In his opinion someone had either forced her into the unnatural position with a great deal of pain, or she had been pushed into that position after death. 'In my opinion,' Dr Wayte stated, 'it was not consistent with a person who had had sex in a normal way.'

Besides questioning the movements of those attending the discotheques that Saturday night, detectives also interviewed taxi drivers, hoteliers and guest house owners in the Colwyn Bay area and investigations soon turned up some clues.

One taxi driver told police that at around 1.15 am on Sunday morning, he had followed a car along Princes Drive and right into Marine Road. The car had then turned off onto waste ground, the site of the old Colwyn Bay Hotel and close to where the body was found. The taxi driver thought the car was either a bronze or brown coloured saloon car, adding that there was a large dog, possibly a Doberman, on the passenger seat.

This was a major lead, as other witnesses had given information which indicated that Karen had been seen walking towards her home at around this time. She was known to have purchased two bags of chips from a take away near the Norfolk House Hotel on Princes Drive, suggesting that she may have already met her killer.

The significance of the brown car took on further importance when a constable reported that he had turned a similar car away from the murder site late on the Sunday afternoon, when curious sightseers had flocked to watch detectives.

A week after the murder police were still no closer to finding the killer and a reconstruction was staged in the hope of jogging the memory of anyone who may have been in the area shortly before the murder.

Chief Superintendent Evans and his officers were shocked at the callousness of many young people who watched the reconstruction as they made their way home after a night out. Several gangs stood jeering as a young police typist, dressed in similar clothes to the victim, followed her last known movements through the resort. 'We are famous, we're on the telly!' one group chanted, while others asked 'Where's Terry Wogan then?' as television crews filmed the events for broadcast on the following day's news bulletins.

It was to be three weeks before police got their man. After making a routine statement, unemployed 31 year old Thomas Ian Harrison, who

Karen Pooley.

lived on Hawarden Road, Colwyn Bay, was taken into custody for further questioning. He was later charged with the murder after admitting that he had met Karen as she walked home alone.

Harrison seemed to be an unlikely suspect in a brutal sex attack: he was disabled with cerebral palsy, and was said to be a bisexual who regularly attended Bible classes.

He made a statement in which he claimed to have met Karen outside Colwyn Bay station after he had driven out in his car, taking his Doberman dog, to post a letter. 'She was sitting on a wall smoking a cigarette and I gave her my coat to keep warm,' he claimed.

Harrison said he returned home, parked the car and set out alone for some fresh air, meeting up with Karen as she made her way home. He asked her if she was enjoying her chips and invited her back to his flat for a cup of coffee, but she refused. He claimed they walked to a bus shelter, where she returned his coat and then asked him if he wanted to have sex. He said that he declined her offer, saying it was cold and he was tired.

They walked on and reached the waste ground, where she told him she wanted to use the toilet. He then alleged that she went behind some bushes and when she returned she was naked from the waist down. He said that she then pulled his trousers down and asked him to have sex. Again he refused. She told him he was use to neither man nor beast and he blacked out and collapsed.

Harrison claimed that he later awoke to find himself on the ground. He ran to the promenade and made his way home. He told officers that he had returned to the waste ground at 2.30 am but could not find Karen and assumed she had gone home.

Detective Inspector Edwards, who had taken the statement, then charged him with the murder and he was remanded in custody pending further investigations.

Thomas Ian Harrison stood trial for murder at Mold Crown Court in January 1987. Mr Justice Mars Jones presided and Harrison pleaded not guilty. Prosecution counsel Mr Alex Carlile QC told the court that Harrison had strangled Karen when she had taunted him after he made an unsuccessful attempt to have sex. He claimed that the accused, a bisexual, had then taken part in an unnatural sex act before strangling from behind. Mr Carlile also claimed that medical evidence would be called to refute any claim of death being anything other than a deliberate act.

It was alleged that Harrison was wearing a pair of women's boots at the time of the attack and that when he returned home he was violently sick. He was also alleged to have gone to his Bible class on the day after committing the murder.

A witness testified that Harrison had claimed to have a hatred of women, after finding his disabled wife in bed with another man. The witness also claimed that Harrison had spoken about finding Karen's body on the night of the murder. He alleged that Harrison had said he had tried to get her to go back to his flat.

A female witness gave evidence that despite claiming to be a homosexual, Harrison also had an active heterosexual sex life. She admitted to having sex with the accused at his flat and that on other occasions he had watched her and another man making love.

His defence counsel, Mr Gareth Edwards, claimed that Harrison had stumbled on top of Karen during a failed attempt to have sex and that in trying to regain his balance he had applied excessive pressure on her neck. He denied that the accused had intentionally strangled her because she had taunted him.

In his closing speech at the end of the six day trial, Mr Carlile alleged that Harrison was a facile liar who continually changed from one version of events to another. He asked the jury to consider the feasibility of the defence's version of events – that Karen Pooley could have met her death by accident. Expert medical evidence suggested this to be impossible.

After listening to the judge's summing up, the jury retired to consider their verdict. They returned to find Harrison guilty of wilful murder and Mr Justice Mars Jones sentenced him to life imprisonment, branding him a 'vicious and dangerous man' and recommending that he serve a minimum of 20 years.

Harrison lodged an appeal against the sentence and six months later this was heard at the Central Appeal Court headed by Mr Justice O'Connor. After listening to evidence supporting the appeal, the judge found in favour of the appellant and on the grounds that the judge had misdirected the jury at the trial the verdict was reduced to one of manslaughter, with a lesser sentence to be determined after psychiatric reports.

Acknowledgements

Several people have helped me during the research and writing of *North Wales Murder Casebook*, and in this respect I am particularly grateful to Wilf Gregg, David Mossop and Matthew Spicer, who all helped during the research stage.

Librarians across North Wales have been unfailing in their willingness to locate and supply relevant material, but in particular Joy Thomas at the Clwyd library, Mold, and Barry Thomas at Gwynedd Archives, Llangefni, both went to great lengths to supply valuable information.

Thanks to the staff at Clwyd Record Office, Ruthin, and the Cheshire Record Office, Chester, who helped with the photographs, and also to staff at the libraries in Flint, Hawarden, Shrewsbury, Aberystwyth, Colindale and Bolton.

Thanks to Alan Parry at North Wales Police for supplying information on the development of the force; to Trevor Roden, photographic manager at the *Chester Chronicle*, for granting me permission to use *Chronicle* photographs; and to Fred Williams at the *Wrexham Leader*. I would also like to thank Arnie Etchells, Robert Brown and Alan Davies, the other 'Lost Boys', and Carla Mann and Lesley Brown for their help with photographs and other illustrations.

We have tried to trace copyright holders of all pictures used, but apologise if we have inadvertently contravened any existing copyright.

I would also like to thank Nicholas and Suzanne Battle and David Graves at Countryside Books, for showing faith and helping me put together my second book in the Murder Casebook series.

Finally, I would like to thank Lisa Moore for her constant support and help in every step from proofreading to researching and for her help with the photography.

Index